SAN FRANCISCO
BY NIGHT

Frommer's

SAN FRANCISCO
by Night

BY

JOE BROWN

WITH

JACK BOULWARE
AND TYLER DAVIDSON

A BALLIETT & FITZGERALD BOOK

MACMILLAN • USA

a disclaimer

Prices fluctuate in the course of time, and travel information changes under the impact of the varied and volatile factors that influence the travel industry. Neither the author nor the publisher can be held responsible for the experiences of readers while traveling. Readers are invited to write to the publisher with ideas, comments, and suggestions for future editions.

about the authors

East Coast transplant **Joe Brown** wrote about nightlife and pop culture for the *Washington Post* for 15 years and is still getting used to feeling like the oldest person in the nightclub. After nearly a year in San Francisco, he's now a hypercaffeinated insomniac and looks forward to a lifetime of exploring the sights, sounds, smells, and tastes of his unpredictable new hometown.

Johnny Huston and **Jeffery Kennedy** contributed to The Club Scene and The Arts.

Jack Boulware, who contributed The Bar Scene, writes a column for *S.F. Weekly*. His writing has appeared in *Playboy, British Esquire,* and *HotWired*. He is a recipient of the Michael R. Batty award for excellence in journalism.

Tyler Davidson, who contributed the Sports chapter, is an associate editor at Reed Travel Features. His work runs regularly in *Travel Weekly* and *TravelAge*.

Balliett & Fitzgerald, Inc.
Executive editor: Tom Dyja
Managing editor: Duncan Bock
Associate editor: Howard Slatkin
Assistant editor: Maria Fernandez
Editorial assistant: Brooke Holmes

Macmillan Travel art director: Michele Laseau

All maps © Simon & Schuster, Inc.

MACMILLAN TRAVEL
A Simon & Schuster Macmillan Company
1633 Broadway
New York, NY 10019

ISBN 0-02-861129-2
ISSN 1088-4696

special sales

Bulk purchases (10+ copies) of Frommer's Travel Guides are available to corporations at special discounts. The Special Sales Department can produce custom editions to be used as premiums and/or for sales promotions to suit individual needs. Existing editions can be produced with custom cover imprints such as corporate logos. For more information write to: Special Sales, Simon & Schuster, 1633 Broadway, New York, NY 10019.

Manufactured in the United States of America

contents

San Francisco Orientation

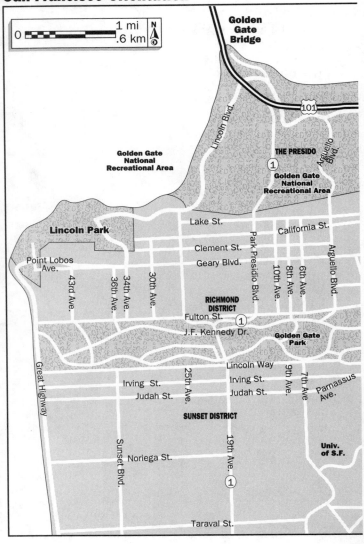

Parc 55 Hotel
55 · Cyril Magnin
Union Sq.

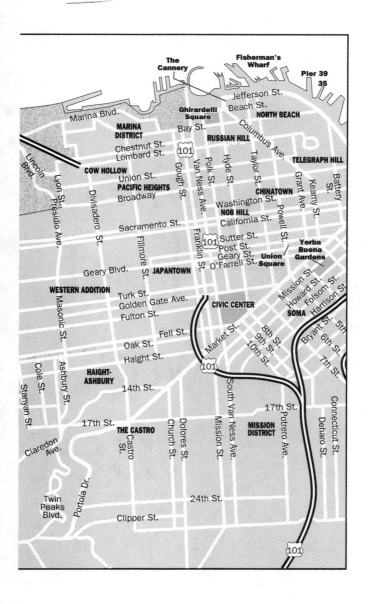

what's
hot,
what's
not

San Francisco is quite a place. Nobody even blinks—not even tourists—when they walk by a doughnut shop at midnight and see a redheaded neophyte drag queen in royal blue sequins picking out crullers. This is a town where anyone, in any outfit—from feathers to Dockers—will feel in the swing of things, as if they really belong.

During my research for this book, I found myself at concerts at the famous Fillmore and Warfield; poked around a sex club (I bumped into an acquaintance—where is Miss Manners when you really need her?); walked along the ocean under the stars, and discovered the nighttime essence of San Francisco's many distinctive neighborhoods—and their denizens.

Though it's by no means a nonstop city like Manhattan or L.A., that's not the point here. Going out in San Francisco is more than just another alternative to being bored. In fact, it's a part of what lured many residents here in the first place. Consequently, night life in this town is pursued with both great focus and creative abandon.

What's hot

Gender blending... It's a gay old town, but the new thing in clubbing is blurring the previously drawn lines between straights and gays, girls, and boys (ethnic and cultural diversity is a given here). Eclecticism is the rule at clubs like **Baby Judy's Discotheque and Leisure Lounge** at Casanova and the friendly Latin dance palace **El Rio** (which affectionately calls itself "Your Dive") in the Mission. See someone you like? Talk to them—who knows? (See The Club Scene and The Bar Scene.)

Hideouts... Everyone's looking for that neighborhood hole in the wall, where no one would ever think of looking for you—and even if they did, they probably couldn't find you because it's so dark and murky. Some choice dives: **Dalva** in the Mission is ultracrowded, straight hipsters, free jukebox. **Specs** is a classic, hard-drinking, chess-playing, Irish music–blasting hideaway in North Beach, with ancient relics from the sea hanging everywhere (and then there's the decor!)—a very hard drinking bar. (See The Bar Scene.)

Deejay deification... The deejay is god in San Francisco. Well to the clubgoers, anyway. This city lives to dance,

dance, dance, and there's plenty of roomy, attitude-free (well, less attitude than you'll find in any other major city) places to twirl, with a bumper crop of winner spinners, including mixtress Page Hodel at **The Box**, Jerry Bonham at **V/SF**, Phil B. at **Pleasuredome**, and Pete Avila at **Sound Factory**. Meanwhile at the Thursday night Lift club at South of Market's **DV8**, deejays David Harness and Aaron O go deep, deeper, deepest into industrial house. (See The Club Scene.)

Retro... These *are* the good old days. So let's do the time warp again: Swing back to the roaring twenties at the subterranean speakeasy **Cafe Du Nord** in the Castro, then flash forward to the thirties at **Bix** (see Late Night Dining) in the Financial District, where grade-A bartender Alan Cohen shakes the city's meanest martini amid luxuriant Art Deco surroundings. At the Haight's **Club Deluxe**, you can step into a full-blown retro-swing dancing scene; the slick, sleek habitués strain to look "regular"—how guys and dolls in the forties looked. Everyone's in sharkskin suits and sipping fancy cocktails, listening to the club's frighteningly good Sinatra sound-alike. At **Julie's Supper Club** in the South of Market nightclub ghetto, every night is like a fifties frat party. To relive the sixties, check out a concert at the reopened **Fillmore Auditorium**, or just pop into any coffeeshop on Haight Street. The seventies ride again at SOMA's **DNA Lounge**, which turns into a disco inferno on Friday nights; and in the Mission, **Baby Judy's Discotheque and Leisure Lounge** (see The Club Scene), a playpen for klub kids infatuated with irony and trash culture, brings back the perhaps-best-forgotten hits of the eighties. Which brings us to...

The Future... S.F.'s South of Market district is home to the famous "Multimedia Gulch" where multimillions are made in the computer-game industry; and with Silicon Valley just down I-280 a bit, the city is a nighttime haven for sleepless computer nerds. You'll find Net-linked computers in cafes like **Muddy Waters** in the Mission, **Brain Wash** in SOMA, **Horseshoe Coffeehouse** in the Haight, and others around town. And diners stand in line to go online at **Icon Byte Bar & Grill**, a wired, weird SOMA eat spot with live music, "smart" martinis, and spicy American/Caribbean fusion food. (See The Cafe Scene and Late Night Dining.)

White trash chic... The I-look-like-I-grew-up-in-a-trailer-park scene is big stuff in many cities with otherwise sane taste, possibly because it's a hoot for terminally hip young urbanites to try to achieve the perfect fashion mix of Nina Hagen and Ellie May Clampett. But in San Francisco, there's a slight hitch: Many of the young habitués of the scene are the real thing; they've seen the inside of more than one double-expando, having grown up in Stockton, Fresno, and other central California farm towns. What you get at their dives of choice—**Chameleon** and **Zeitgeist** (see The Club Scene and The Bar Scene), for instance, on opposite ends of Valencia Street—is a blend of Budweiser, beehive babes, and bikers, kicking up their heels to bands like the White Trash Debutantes, a punky, all-female alternative rock band that would do their cocktail-waitress mamas proud.

Sex... Long before Madonna discovered it, San Franciscans were making pleasure an art and a way of life—many people have migrated here just so they can do exactly what they want and find someone (or many) to do it with. People here tend to wear their insides on their outsides, so you can tell at a glance just what scene they're into, from leather on. Of course, AIDS and other attendant dangers have made people more cautious than they were in the famously free-for-all San Francisco sixties and seventies, but horniness is the true mother of invention, and San Francisco still swings at night—people have come up with ingenious ways to get some without getting anything. There's a thriving sex club scene, epitomized by the spanking-clean and monitored **Eros** club for gay men near the Castro, and the anything- and anyone-goes five-floor South of Market sexual amusement park called the **Playground** for men and women, straights, gays, and whatever else you can come up with. Wednesday's Bondage-a-Go-Go night at SOMA's cavernous and otherwise punky **Trocadero** club is packed with suburban swingers, swappers, and scenesters. (See The Club Scene.) And there are plenty of witty, unabashed sex shops like the Mission's women-owned-and-operated **Good Vibrations**, a clean, well-lighted place to buy a dildo—there's even a vibrator museum. (See Hanging Out.)

What's not

High-profile, big-scene clubs... If you see a line of eager young club-hoppers lined up on the sidewalk, all dressed down and hoping the bouncer will like their looks and motion them inside, run the other way. You are either in a very bad nightmare or at a hopelessly out-of-date South of Market club packed with the bridge-and-tunnel crowd. The hottest clubs shun publicity in any form, often changing their names weekly to evade attention-getting reviews in local entertainment guides. These new "hit-and-run" bars aren't xenophobic or unkind to strangers, they simply want to avoid the publicity overkill that turned the once-hip South of Market scene into an overcrowded magnet for suburban wannabes. To find the hippest bars and clubs, go to a neighborhood cafe that appeals to you, and ask the wait staff.

Slammers, depth charges, Jell-O shots... Or any other alcoholic concoction designed strictly to get you smashed in a nanosecond. That includes the perpetual favorite of the underage set known as the Long Island Iced Tea. Those instant-idiot potions have been replaced by sophisticated cocktails—martinis, Rob Roys, and the exceptionally popular Cosmopolitan (vodka with cranberry and lime juice—stirred, not shaken). To find out the latest cocktails and the hottest bartenders in the Bay Area, get to a computer and check out the **http://www.hotwired.com/cocktail/** website.

Grunge anything... Send those Doc Martens and that stringy hair back to Seattle where it belongs. San Francisco has come to its senses. Gone for now are those droopy flannel shirts and cutoff overalls. They've been replaced by several other equally questionable fashion trends, including the fifties housewife look—shirtwaist dresses that were cute on "I Love Lucy," but are a bit too close to the sixties earth-mother mode in the current thrift-store version—and vintage athletic wear, ranging from pre-Spandex warm-up suits to high-school basketball jerseys.

Thai food for every meal... A person can only eat so much spicy peanut sauce, after all. The obsession with Thai food has given way to a love affair with tapas, Spanish "little dishes" that tend to be found in hip, crowded neighborhood joints like **Cha Cha Cha** in the Haight. (See Late Night Dining.)

Baseball by the stars... Night games at **Candlestick** have never been hot. In fact, they've been so cold that every fan who stayed until the end of an extra-inning game was given a "Croix de Candlestick" badge that featured the Giants' logo dripping with icicles. Go if you must, but plan to freeze. The only thing more unhot than the weather is the widely detested new name for the stadium: 3Com Park. It's so bad that the *San Francisco Chronicle* refuses to use it in print. (See Sports.)

Raunchy North Beach strip joints... You know it's over when the Condor—former home of Carol Doda, San Francisco's most infamous breast-barer—has been turned into a corner coffeehouse. But all is not lost. Bawdy strip joints with barkers at the door may be a thing of the past, but nude bodies are still in full supply at places like **Centerfolds**, an upscale limos-and-lap-dancing club where dancers who look like models or Las Vegas showgirls earn four figures a night to strut their stuff, often for well-heeled celebrities. (See The Club Scene.)

the clu

b scene

1

Here's a night out in San Francisco: On the SRO floor of the Great American Music Hall, you're sandwiched between a Fortysomething fellow who has dyed what little

hair he has left purple (his beard, too) and a pair of alterna-
tive-loving nuns from Berkeley. Sixty-year-old Yoko Ono is
wailing onstage, with her twenty-year-old son, Sean, on guitar and a drop-by Beastie Boy on bass. The whole thing is
being filmed for CD-ROM, and you all have to keep duck-
ing when the camera crane swings over your heads.
Armistead Maupin, author of the famous "Tales of the City"
books chronicling another age of San Francisco, watches
benevolently from the balcony with his lover, Terry, which
makes you feel like you're a character in his next book. Which
you probably are. On the bus home, two neo-hippy girls
engage a trio of happy winos in a delightedly snarky conversation about the vocal merits of Yoko Ono and how men only
want sex. Meanwhile, drag nuns are hosting a show featuring
"Ethel Merman," "Luciano Pavarotti" and a tiny drag queen
who gyrates over audience member "Vanessa Williams." Back
outside, a gaggle of clucking, cawing fuschia-and-purple drag
chickens are racing up and down Castro Street, urging you to
elect a man "Empress of San Francisco."

"San Francisco is the town where white kids go to die," a
young friend of ours remarked before decamping to the
cleaner and healthier streets of Los Angeles. And it's true;
take the Mission, for example. Legions of tattooed white
zombies seem to rise at noon after a night of clubbing, head
out to Muddy Waters (see The Cafe Scene) for a latte before
a serious afternoon of zine study. These people like to rock. If
nothing else, San Francisco has an audience for unsigned
bands—an audience that cares.

The Bay Area is also a choice stop for big names on
national tours, and the city is a magnet for creative musical
people, so there's always several choices for live music every
night of the week. The city continues to spawn a rich array of
homegrown musical acts, with devoted local followings—
insular San Francisco doesn't much care if it's home team players break out and become "the next Huey Lewis." Even dance
clubs often mix it up with appearances by live performers.
Homegrown names to watch for include drag dance diva
Pussy Tourette, acid-jazzers Broun Fellinis, the somber,
acoustic-rock Red House Painters, ace lesbian Elvis impersonator Elvis Herselvis, serious singer/songwriter Mark Eitzel,
and the queercore (aggressive, funny hardcore punk made by
and for young queers) stars Pansy Division and Tribe 8.

Unlike the city's 10,000 or so bars, most dance clubs usually operate just one night a week. And there's usually a cover

charge, from cheapish to steepish. Of course, you CAN dance in San Francisco bars (actually, you can do almost anything you can think of in bars here—and then someone will show up to show you something you haven't even thought of), but sometimes you want that Total Club Experience. You know: Will-I-get-in? (often combined with How-do-I-look?) anxiety, eternal coat-check lines, bartenders who go "blind" when *you* reach the bar, elitist deejays, perfect people with attitude... Why do you think people do all those drugs at clubs?

Actually, you'll find San Francisco clubs unusually welcoming (especially of the unusual) and relatively attitude-free. And so many people go out, and stay out so late, you may wonder if anyone in this city has a real job.

The trend in S.F. is toward chameleon clubs—a place has one name (and one distinctive crowd) tonight and another name and crowd tomorrow night. Even more than in most cities, the S.F. club scene is in a constant state of change—it's a series of fabulous one-night stands. A popular weekly nightspot in January is likely to be a memory (for those who still have enough brain cells to retain memories) by June.

A denizen of the S.F. nightclub scene named Miss Polly has self-published a fascinating book called *I Found God at The End Up*, sort of a *Celestine Prophecy* for the after-midnight club crowd. In the true spirit (well, one of the true spirits) of San Francisco, it's a look at nightlife as a venue for spiritual transformation and possibilities. She offers sensible guidelines for those who plan to take leave of their senses: "Don't gossip. Be polite. Tip well. In a noisy bar, don't try to talk or make introductions. Just smile, wave, and dance. Move in time to the music, and you can walk gracefully through any crowd. Communicate clearly (e.g., 'I'm going to the hotel for a nap/shower'; 'I'm having an anxiety attack and will see you later'; 'I require the paramedics,' etc.). Know when to leave, which is when you're not having fun anymore."

Thanks, Miss Polly. We have a few more tips: On Fridays, check out the cooler coffeeshops, record, book, and vintage-clothing stores for fliers and invitation cards to bars, clubs, and parties—the corner of Castro and Market is also a good spot for these handouts. Many of these fliers offer discounts or even free admission before a certain hour. Often you can get in free before 10pm, get your hand stamped, go out and come back later. Another good information resource is the Be-At Line (tel 415/626–4087), a handy hotline detailing the best current spots for dancing, emphasizing hip-hop, jazz, and soul.

SAN FRANCISCO ◡ THE CLUB SCENE

A fun way to explore S.F. clubs while you party safely is the **3 Babes & a Bus** club tour (tel 415/552–2582; Fridays and Saturdays, reservations required, participants must be 21 or over). Hostesses Paula Sabatelli, Donna Lo Cicero, and Susan Francke load their very mixed group (it might be a scramble of suburban twentysomethings and surprisingly hip Hadassah ladies) onto a fully-stocked party bus, and head off to a full menu of city clubs—the list changes nightly. There are no cover charges, you receive priority admittance (if you want to return to a particular club later that night, you'll be admitted free), one free drink during the night, and maybe you even make some new pals to go clubbing with in the future.

Sources

Plenty of restaurants present live music, and neighborhood bars and cafes often present local acts for free. Most of the major dance clubs are situated in the South of Market (SOMA) industrial area, also home to the highly hyped Multimedia Gulch. But you'll find live music venues sprinkled throughout the city. To keep up with the latest listings, check the *San Francisco Chronicle*, the free weekly alternatives *SF Weekly* and *Bay Guardian*, and the free monthly *BAM (Bay Area Music)* magazine.

Now we don't want to sound like your mother, but we just have to remind you of a few more things: Always call ahead to find out who's playing and how much it costs (not to mention if the club still exists: Many of the places listed here have stood the test of time, but we've included a handful of fun fly-by-night evenings that may have changed their spots by the time you read this). Bring a jacket (don't take our word for it, ask anyone; you can check it at coat check). And finally: Always bring your ID to prove you're 21 or over. Even if you're over 30. Have fun, dears.

Who to See and Hear

Here's a selective, A-to-Z shortlist of bands, performers, and personalities to watch out for:

Alphabet Soup: One of the first Bay Area bands to mix hip-hop and jazz.

Anibade and Ledisi. Anibade has a great, funky horn sound; Ledisi is a fiery, soulful singer with a social conscience.

Bambi Lake and Veronica Klaus: Transsexual chanteuses—Lake is all over the map; Klaus specializes in jazzy blues.

Barbara Manning/SF Seals: Indie queen with deadpan wit and voice, who many feel paved the way for Liz Phair and others.

The Billy Nayer Show: Punk cabaret with comedy and psychotic performance art.

The Billy Tipton Memorial Quartet: All-female crew with New Orleans jazz and jump sound (named for the famous jazzman who was discovered to be a jazzwoman after his death).

Broun Fellinis: Bay Area acid-jazz veterans.

Charlie Hunter Trio: S.F.'s best-known acid-jazz figure, an eight-string guitar virtuoso.

Elvis Herselvis: Terrific lesbian Elvis impersonator, usually backed by the Straight White Men.

Frenchy: Arguably S.F.'s best lounge-music act; their repertoire includes the "Spider Man" theme song.

The Hi-Fives: Bay area mod rock at its best (and most handsome).

James T. Kirk: Major label acid-jazzers.

Jawbreaker: Thinking man's Green Day; pop punk with extended, noisy, instrumental segues.

Jill Tracy: Spooky solo piano chanteuse.

Juan Escovedo: A member of the musical Escovedo family fronts a ten-piece salsa band.

Los Angelitos: A twelve-piece that mixes jazz, Latin, and funk sounds.

Mark Eitzel: A master of melancholy to rival Morrissey. Hear him and weep.

Midnight Voices: Eclectic hip-hop that aims to make you think and boogie; starring Mohammed from MTV's "The Real World."

Mirv: Punk rock played by men in old-fogy golf clothes who groan for Geritol between songs.

The Mr. T Experience: Fast, short, catchy punk songs.

Mudd People: They invade public spaces and events totally covered in mud and dripping everywhere. Why not?

Orang Mancinis: Henry Mancini tribute band, featuring Joe Gore (who plays with P. J. Harvey and Tom Waits) and horn supremo Ralph Carney.

Pansy Division: Jokey, silly, perpetually horny homo pop-punk.

Patsy Cline and the Memphis G-Spots: Campy country drag outfit.

Pete Escovedo: Sheila E's dad, and a 25-year veteran of Latin jazz whose shows are often family affairs.

Preacher Boy and the Natural Blues: Preacher Boy plays the banjo, croons, and makes (some of) the crowd swoon.

Pussy Tourette: Wickedly funny dance-rock drag diva.

Red House Painters: Incredibly slow, incredibly sad acoustic/electric ballads—music to commit suicide by.

Richard Bruckner: Critically celebrated singer/songwriter with world-weary voice and literate lyrics.

Rinde Eckert: Chrome-domed solo performer who veers from country to Gregorian chants.

Simone White Quartet: Versatile drummer's jazz quartet.

Souls of Mischief: Hip-hop with complex lyrics, old-school ambience.

Stone Fox: Trashy, noisy California glam, adorned in sequins and feather boas.

Susie Sounds: See her for free any night in front of the Castro Wells Fargo ATM, singing ballads in a high, spooky "Twin Peaks" voice. You can't miss her—she's the one with the accordion and the winged helmet with a blinking red light on top.

Tarnation: Excellent neo-country featuring Paula Frazer's Southern Gothic lyrics and lilting Patsy Cline–esque vocals.

The Trash Women: Garage-rocking gals in skimpy outfits.

Tribe 8: Dyke rock with a West Coast hardcore punk sound. Lead singer Lynn Breedlove is a white-trash hybrid of Patti Smith and Jim Morrison.

X-Tal: Agit-rock doesn't get any smarter or crankier than this four-piece with three singers, two male and one female.

The Lowdown

The clubland circuit (24 hours, 7 days)... The club week begins on Saturday at an enormous South of Market industrial warehouse that houses the primo S.F. dance club **Club Townsend**, still going strong halfway through its first decade. On Saturday night, it hosts **Club Universe**, which attracts party people of all ages, races, genders, and orientations; there's a new decor every week (awesome, really, when you consider the size and scope of the makeover) and live performances. Come Sunday night the same space turns into the primarily (and primally) gay **Pleasuredome**, packed to the rafters with some 2,000 muscle boys. If you're looking for that Studio 54-esque shirts-off, speed-frenzied, hip-pumping orgy with plenty of beefcake watching, this is the place. A nightly highlight is when the spinning, circular "drug light" descends to eye level at one point, spinning and blinding the already delirious dancers. A lowlight is at 2am, when bouncers walk through the club snatching the drinks right out of your hand. But you can switch to water, soda, or Gatorade as the sound turns into tweaky, repetitive, shall we say "crystalline" music. The beat goes on till 7am, and if you're still not done, head for **The End Up**, where everyone ends up sooner or later. Usually later. For those who refuse to let go of the weekend, a club called Rehab (at **The Pit**, 9th St. and Howard St.) opens at 5:30am Monday morning. Eeuuuuuwww.

When last we checked, the weekday circuit looked like this: Mondays move to the self-explanatory Funk Night at a cozy and comfortable old gay bar, **The Stud**; Tuesdays, it's back to The Stud for the house-y Phat Free; Wednesdays is a tie between the fabulously eccentric X-athon **Baby Judy's Discotheque and Leisure Lounge** in the Mission and the gal-centric **Faster Pussycat!** Now and (we hope) forever, Thursdays belong to **The Box**. The essential club of all S.F. clubs, The Box is a perennial Thursday night affair going strong since the late eighties. If you want to pose, cruise, booze, or schmooze, go someplace else. The Box is where San Francisco (straight and gay) comes to dance. Period. In its stripped-down, unpretentious South of Market warehouse space, you'll see all the new moves first, with a high-energy mix of boys and girls, straight and gay, black/white/Latin/Asian.... It doesn't really matter what you look like, just as long as you keep it moving. Après Box, it's fun to play pinball and dance to the likes of Foreigner's "Cold As Ice" at the seriously pounding White Trash at **The Stud**. Friday's children—huge numbers of them from all over the Bay Area—go to twirl to house, techno, and funk at the multilevel **Sound Factory** South of Market.

Which brings us back around again to Saturday. Yippee.

Straight-up dance fever... For many straight folks in San Francisco, dancing is less about celebrating than reinforcing status. So in the city's predominantly straight nightclubs (almost no place is 100 percent pure either way), you're likely to find more couples, more attitude, more emphasis on style, and less diversity. By and large, you'll also find better deejays. Known as San Francisco's rave HQ since the scene's early-nineties heyday, South of Market's **The End Up** still attracts a young, freakish, after-hours crowd that's into hallucinogens and trance music. Not much needs to be said about it: This is The Place. (A tip from Miss Polly: "Order drinks in plastic cups. Tip $1 with each drink. If the bartender knocks on the counter, your drink is free. Tip anyway if you want this to happen again.") The club's all-day Sunday "tea dance" is a choice way to chill after a night spent tweaking under a strobe light. It begins at 6am and goes on all day and evening, with dancing indoors and out on the deck amid eucalyptus trees, a waterfall, and live conga drummers.

With its dress code (no sneakers, hooded sweats, or baseball caps), **Sound Factory** tries to dissuade gang members and disruptive elements from crashing the party. This multilevel, 15,000-square-foot South of Market discotheque dishes up house, techno, and funk, attracting well-groomed booty shakers from all over the

Bay Area. Internationally renowned deejays, like Frankie Knuckles and Little Louis Vega, have been known to spin here on occasion.

The cavernous **DV8**, owned by actor Rob Schneider, the once-and-always "Saturday Night Live" making-copies guy, offers four more floors of fun South of Market (experience the six-way digital sound system!), featuring industrial, funk, and house. The faux-tropical Brazilian disco **Bahia Cabana**, in Hayes Valley, mixes straight and gay dancers in a tasty blend of live salsa music, house, and techno nightclub action. Sunday is the big night at the city's premiere singles bar, **Johnny Love's** in Polk Gulch; but any night of the week this swanky safari-themed fern bar with a restaurant and dance club is where uptown boy goes to meet upscale girl. And vice versa. At the Mission's **Plastik** (as in plastik people), the elite meet to feel even more elite. It's a gathering place for dressed-up (coked-up?) male and female supermodels and wannabes. If guest list hierarchies are important to your self-validation, here's your mecca.

Queer disco inferno... Devastated by AIDS, gays and lesbians in San Francisco spent most of the eighties caregiving and grieving, and the city's once-thriving nightclub scene all but vanished. The nineties, however, have seen a real resurgence, perhaps because gays and lesbians have learned how invaluable celebrating life is. And, true to the community's diverse nature, there's something for everyone.

Gay folks who could care less about making a scene or trolling for dates and just want to dance go to Thursday's **The Box**, just like everybody else. For the scene makers, especially the guys, the weekend's Club Universe and Pleasuredome at **Club Townsend** is the biggest gay disco scene—biggest dance floor, biggest sound system, biggest cover charge, biggest pecs. But there are plenty of alternatives every night of the week.

The Stud, with its cozy, woody decor, rates low on the attitude barometer and is one of the city's oldest and friendliest dance bars. Gays and lesbians of all shapes and sizes flock here to bump and grind on a teeny dance floor, where Janis Joplin herself was once spotted shaking it. Watch for the red laser light near the dance floor that transmits "subliminal" messages to the dancers' peripheral vision. The Stud's constantly changing theme nights—recent additions include Trannyshack, a dragstravaganza on Tuesday nights, and Poontown, a grrrlie punk party on Saturday nights—keep it hip. Cheap covers, chummy bartenders and an electric train chugging over the bar are added pluses. Similar in scale is **The Cafe**, the only coed dance bar in the Castro. The crowd that lines up each weekend to get into this well-placed neon-and-mirrors haunt is a bit dressy, and the music more pop than house, heavy on the divas. There's dancing every night of the week, but the best spot is off the floor and out on the balcony, where you can sip a cocktail and look down on the crowds converging from Market and Castro Streets.

If your most nightmarish vision of a gay disco is a roomful of wax-chested, thick-necked, 'roid-pumped, and mood-enhanced ravers flexing to thumpa-thumpa music, **Baby Judy's Discotheque and Leisure Lounge** (Wednesdays at the Mission's Casanova) is a possible dream come true. In a word: kooky. Deejays Alvin-a-Go-Go and Deena Davenport are kitsch connoisseurs, and decades of severe pop-culture damage have spawned a fun and freakish sensibility. Most of the music is twisted and retro and by white people, from Yma Sumac/Nina Haagen shrieking to TV and movie themes; the Deejays often leave the booth to dance among the crowd, and the records skip now and then. The crowd—male, female, undecided—is oddball and proud, more interested in silly clothes than perfect bodies. **V/SF** is another answered prayer: a no-smoking dance club. Designed in response to community polls on health-consciousness, the clean, classy club near the civic center aims to please by keeping all smoking outside and promoting community unity within while lights flash and discs spin. The prohibition on tobacco doesn't mean the patrons aren't putting *other* things in their bodies, but at least clothes don't smell when you get home. Contrary to the club's everyone-is-welcome ads, the clientele is predominantly male, and the cover charge is steep. However, Saturday nights it hosts the girl-centric dance party called G-Spot, hosted by Deejay Downtown Donna, for everyone from suburban preppy lesbians to severe scenestresses.

The eclectic and polysexual frontier... Every other Saturday, a predominantly Latino crowd moves to Latino house in the friendly **Futura**, set in a huge SOMA warehouse with balcony and looooong bar. Deejays Raymundo and Rubin create their own version of Latino house, mixing cumbias and merengues with programmed beats. Dominated by tough dykes, the weekly **Faster Pussycat!** in the Mission takes its name from the fab Russ Meyer flick about murderous, bodacious go-go dancers on the lam. Most nights feature two or three female rock bands, usually local. Between sets, Downtown Donna spins techno, funk, and rock. Drunken bike messengers add an obnoxious element to the site, which has two rooms, one for drinking and playing pool, the other for dancing and rocking. **Litterbox** is the latest twisted offering from scene maven Michael Blue, a major force behind Club Uranus and other early-nineties queer nightspots. The boys–locker room dirty sweatiness of Blue's previous club, Fiend, has been toned down a bit. A pair of deejays—Javier (male) and Junkyard (female)—spin glam, punk, funk, and more. The monthly **Dragstrip** combines two S.F. institutions; drag and sex work for double the polymorphous perversity, with strippers doing drag shows and drag queens all but stripping. On this stage, the city's more clever courtesans of all sexes become performance artists. The free-for-all at Dragstrip is completely participatory, with the equally decked-out dance crowd often outshining the performers—fitting for a town that boasts its own prostitutes league, known as Coyote. Heterosexuals with a craving for kink might enjoy Bondage-a-Go-Go, a weekly event at the **Trocadero**.

Best deejays... From her "Temple of Boom," Page Hodel rocks **The Box** (Thursday nights) with an accessible, high-energy house/club music mix. She's got all the very latest stuff, but keeps the kids squealing by generously mixing in familiar tracks from the seventies and eighties. The megaclubs **Sound Factory**, **Club Universe**, and **Pleasuredome** claim the city's best and imported talent, like the Sound Factory's Pete Avila. Universe/Pleasuredome boasts Hodel and fellow turntable talents David Harness and Phil B. The deejays at **The Stud** take the seventies and eighties seriously, especially at the Sunday night eighties party. The Bay Area's best-known world-music deejay, Cheb I Sabbah, has a longstanding weekly gig at **Nickie's BBQ**, a normally funk-dominated Lower

Haight site. Sounds from Africa, the Middle East, and Asia melt and meld into one another during one of his typical sets. And finally, what the klub kids at **Baby Judy's Discotheque and Leisure Lounge** lack in mixing finesse, they make up for with their getups and enthusiasm.

Alt.rock on the turntable... As one veteran S.F. band (and they're still around, as the Cybership) put it long ago: "We built this city on rock and roll." And it's still true: There are two handfuls of dependable dance clubs spinning heavy-duty rock. The Mission's cramped and dingy **Chameleon Club**, whose best feature is the colorful, tacky Keane-style thriftshop paintings tacked to the wall, used to be headquarters for out-of-town indie bands; now it's booking more deejays and fewer bands, with spoken-word shows on Monday nights. The great 'n' grungy **DNA Lounge** in SOMA is a fun, funky, no-frills place to dance to rock and roll. **Miss Pearl's Jam House** is a Caribbean-themed restaurant and club where you can eat jerked Jamaican food and watch for touring rock stars, who often stay at the adjoining Phoenix Hotel. The only-eighties music club, **New Wave City**, is one of those nomadic clubs, meaning it's in a different venue every month, and with a different theme each time: One night it's a Morrissey mope-along, the next it's a John Hughes Appreciation Night, or a Go-Gos party where drag queens compete against genetic females in a go-go contest (Surprise! The real girls won this one). Watch for flyers. Atmosphere is not a consideration at the Haight's grimy, dark **Nightbreak**, a rough rock-and-roller bar where the seventies-rawk attire of black leather jacket, big hair, and no shirt (eeeeew!) is de rigueur.

In the cradle of acid jazz... Take your basic straight-ahead jazz and stir in more beat-driven sounds—hip-hop, funk, R&B—and you have acid jazz. The Bay Area is perhaps the best-known national spot for this heady concoction, producing renowned practitioners like Blue Note recording artists the Charlie Hunter Trio (who recently added a second saxman and became a quartet). Live acts play at many spots around town. Here's a fun fact: One of the first S.F. supper clubs for the rich and beautiful, **330 Ritch**, was a seventies-era hardcore sex club. Try that as a conversation starter next time you're in the very bland and very beige restaurant half of the warehouse-style club; then try it again when you move into the cold, hard, sleek-surfaced dance bar, which hosts parties for *Wired* magazine and other smart-set sorts. It draws a snazzy acid-jazz crowd on weekends; during the week, less formal but equally beautiful hip-hop devotees congregate to enjoy its wine bar, cigar bar, dining room, and a pay phone strategically located in one of the noisiest areas. The unpretentious **Elbo Room** in the Mission district showcases many of the same acid-jazz acts in its unventilated upstairs room (the bluish downstairs bar is just for drinkin' and yakkin'), but this time they're playing for Mission hipsters and other people who don't mind sweating. The Charlie Hunter Trio named a song on its Blue Note album "bing, bing, bing!" after this neighborhood fixture; the Broun Fellinis and other renowned local musicians play here frequently. When there's no band, a deejay spins hip-hop and classic James Brown funk. A small jazz/ambient/performance catchall on Market Street, **Cafe du Nord** styles itself as a twenties-or thirties- style underground speakeasy, more retro than modern, and a large percentage of its crowd enjoys dressing the part. The posh, pretty-people-filled **Up & Down Club** is a relatively new, supermodel-friendly South of Market hangout—that's because it's part-owned by supermodel Christy Turlington (one of the nice ones).

Yes, Dorothy, they still have raving... To escape the hassles with cops, and keep everyone involved safe and comfortable, the city's once-ravenous rave scene has pretty much packed up and moved indoors to established warehouse-style clubs like **Sound Factory**, where raves are one-nighters. Check for fliers, invites and the free West Coast deejay–scene magazine *XLR8* at record stores and cool coffeeshops, including Housewares, at 1322 Haight.

Big rock halls... Like punk never happened. It's sad but true: S.F.'s biggest rock sites still have a sixties atmosphere, even when the bands playing are the sort who make a show of hating hippies. The legacy of promoter Bill Graham lives on at the city's largest rock venue, the multi-tiered **Warfield**, which recently presented related-across-time banshees Bjork and Yoko Ono. Patrons can sit at tables or stand in the small area close to the stage, where cocktail waitresses steer drink trays through shoulder-to-shoulder crowds. The security people all look like refugees from the Summer of Love, and age brings out their fascistic tendencies. Arrive early, buy a drink, and find a comfortable spot to watch the show; we heartily recommend staying off the floor and sitting in the front balcony. Here, as at the famous **Fillmore**, you're free to chat through the show. Though reminiscent of a grandiose high school auditorium, the Fillmore is much more friendly and comfortable; the sound tends to be better as well. The sixties refuse to die at this recently refurbished ballroom-style hall—we recently witnessed a sold-out show by Donovan, which flushed cobweb-covered hippies out of hiding from their yurts in Marin. As in days of yore, a big bowl of trademark red apples sits in the front lobby, and those who desire something more than horsey food can dine and drink upstairs in a room decorated with acid-inspired vintage concert posters. More wide than long, the ground floor is spacious; it's usually easy to stake out a good spot. Upstairs, the balconies are far off to the sides, but they do offer tables and chairs.

Of the midsized clubs, the modestly named **Great American Music Hall**, which looks just like what it used to be—a bordello—is most enjoyable, though the staff can be rude and pushy, emphasizing the eats and drinks over respect for performers onstage. Still, you can get really close to the performers and even run upstairs to the balcony if you feel claustrophobic. Built at the turn of the century, the Great American is an architectural curiosity, and its Tenderloin fringe location, right next door to the Mitchell Brothers' famed porno theater, adds that special dangerous flavor. Thanks to its big-screen TVs and blandly industrial look, Boz Scagg's South of Market rock showcase, **Slim's**, could be an oversized sports bar in Anytown, USA. The sound is average, and it draws well-scrubbed yuppie regulars who like using live rock music as background for their conversations (I wonder if they have anything to talk about AFTER the show). Free-loading music-biz schmoozers make up a large part of the crowd, usually sitting at the tables on the back balcony for the shows, which are heavily skewed toward modern-rock radio and neo-psychedelia. The bar serves food and overpriced drinks. A movie screen descends to obscure the stage between bands, and a few irritatingly placed poles obscure the stage all night long.

Intimate mosh pits and headbanging... Small rock venues are often cheaper and more enjoyable in terms of atmosphere. At the Mission's **DNA Lounge**, if you want to get off the floor and watch the slamming, head for the balcony, where you'll also find the pool tables. Along with nearby **Kilowatt** and Potrero Hill's **Bottom of the Hill**, it draws the best out-of-town bands. Bottom of the Hill often features major-label acts on virgin U.S. tours— before they break bigtime or belly flop—and also hosts Northwest and West Coast indie bands—greasy-haired, hardrocking Seattle trolls, Olympia feminist rock and cuddlecore (cutesy, jangly indie rock fronted by pretty, slightly off girl vocalists), and local punk/pop pranksters. Do not adjust your vision: The decor in this hip, medium-small club out in the middle of nowhere is tilted on purpose, so you feel a bit tipsy even before your first cold one. Kilowatt is a major part of the thriving Mission scene, with consistently strong booking featuring Japanese noise, sixties garage rock, and local/national indie/punk fare. The club's mixed drinks are hearty, the cover charge affordable, and you might be inspired to take a picture of the neon sign. The motormouth alcoholics at the **Chameleon** are capable of ruining a good show, especially if the band doesn't rely on high volume. After a few too many police hassles, the Chameleon has curtailed rock bookings, especially lineups featuring out-of-town acts. The decor is drab, the bathrooms are small, and the regulars—well, their conversations deserve to be drowned out by guitars.

Stranded between strip clubs in North Beach, the Beat-era **Purple Onion** usually hosts surf rockers these days in a kegger-party atmosphere. Purple Onion acts are mostly from the strange SoCal or Japanese surf-punk scenes, and the music is garage-surf, a Beach Boys–meets–Big Daddy Roth kind of thing. Mellower rock acts can be heard sometimes in North Beach at **Bimbo's 365**, one of the last remaining supper clubs from the area's nightspot glory days. With its crimson-scarlet-ruby-red decor and candlelit tables, this forties speakeasy is far and away the most beautiful place to see a rock show and the adult in all of us enjoys the table service and crystal-clear sound system. Bands who book the place may play anything from jazz and lounge music to literate indie rock and soul. The Haight's dark, crowded **Nightbreak** is where you'll see the few remaining hair bands that pass through town, and once in a while a novelty like Panic in Detroit, a Bowie tribute band.

Paradise Lounge in SOMA splits its attention between straight-ahead rock bands, trashy Southern California–based shock rock outfits like the Genitor-turers and Crispen Glover (always a sellout here), and oddities like New York's The Voluptuous Horror of Karen Black. This black-walled maze is also the home of chee-zee lounge lizard the Fabulous Bud E. Luv. With an inside like a cavernous ocean-blue seashell, the **Troca-dero** used to be the city's biggest gay disco, but after years of disuse, it's been reclaimed as the home of everything young and punky, a veritable rock-and-roll high school. (Wear black and big scary boots.) **The Hotel Utah**, a homey, folksy bar in a former hotel where bands rock out unplugged on a postage-stamp-size stage. Local groups like the neo-country Tarnation and alcoholic/romantic Mark Eitzel have played at the Hotel Utah; Oscar-nominated actress Mare Winningham comes in from her out-of-town ranch to play her acoustic music there.

All that jazz and blues... Jazz is alive and well in the city, which has an intimate connection to the music's postwar forms due to its history as a breeding ground for Beat. In fact, city fathers and mothers are pondering developing a neighborhood near Pacific Heights into a jazz theme park. Most S.F. venues program an eclectic mix of music, so you'll catch rock one night, funk the next, and jazz on another. Check the performance lineups at supper and small clubs. Or just take a walk through North Beach, where you're always likely to hear jazz—cool or hot—blowing out of one of the many always-open bar doors. On Columbus, the forties supper club **Bimbo's 365** is the perfect lounge to see one of today's neo-bop acts. For big-name jazz acts, a good bet is always **Kimball's**. This standby books both established jazz greats like song styl-ist Nancy Wilson and young talents like Joshua Redman; most live shows are jazz or R&B, with salsa nights on the weekends. Near some of the city's largest concert halls and toniest restaurants around the Civic Center, the place draws actual rich people, not just bohemians dressing up in vintage and pretending to be rich. Nearby at **Up & Down Club**, South of Market, young jazz acts play downstairs. Housed in the basement of a gigantic "Swiss

Miss" building better suited for the Alps than Market Street, **Cafe Du Nord** showcases many talented up-and-coming local jazz performers. Popular with hepcats, the restuarant **Eleven** serves Italian food with six nights of jazz on the cusp of the Civic Center area. If you want to hear a chanteuse in an intimate setting try **Julie Ring's Heart and Soul**, near Russian Hill. On Folsom, **Julie's Supper Club**'s dark, tropical bar gives onto a dining room that's all bright lights and white surfaces, like a missing deck from the Love Boat. Fans of fruity drinks that look like household cleaners can find aesthetically superior Blue Hawaiians (garnished with plastic swordfish that make excellent hairpins), but the live jazz and R&B—on Fridays and Saturdays—is average, lacking the starpower of Kimball's and the originality found at newer clubs. A down-and-dirty spot for straight-ahead jazz and gutbucket blues is **The Saloon**, a rowdy, always-crowded North Beach joint that also happens to be the oldest surviving bar in the city. It looks and feels like it. Downtown's **The Blue Lamp** is another rare blues refuge. Suitably tight and smoky, this faded beauty of a club is home to a time-warped crowd who are retro down to their suspenders and handbags. Watch for occasional appearances by St. Vitus's Dance, "the Sex Pistols of Swing," who mix amps and horn sections, attracting jitterbuggers and green-haired waifs alike. Those looking for a more otherworldly rhythm should migrate to Hayes Valley's **Bahia Cabana**, where the emphasis is on Brazilian music, with frequent visits from samba bands and dancers, though the place has been suffering an identity crisis lately, trying gay nights and all sorts of short-lived themes.

The retro scene... Do people love retro because they're afraid of the year 2000? One of the more curious trends of recent years is the revival of conservative (but undeniably stylish) forms of fun: San Francisco is overrun with cocktail parties (with real cocktails!), supper clubs, fancy clothes (more often than not from thrift shops, but hey...), and swinging bachelor-pad lounge music by revived oldsters Martin Denny and Esquivel and smarty-pants newcomers Combustible Edison. The S.F. retro scene started at the Red Room (see The Bar Scene) and the Haight's Club Deluxe, both affecting a studiedly conservative, return-to-Eisenhower look and attitude, filtered

SAN FRANCISCO ⟨ THE CLUB SCENE

through nineties irony. It's more a scene than a musical happening. But as more and more Gen Xers discover the joys of martinis and bongos, cabaret is making a comeback (see "Cabaret, real not faux…" below). Although you're not likely to find the stylish ambience immortalized in Hollywood films from the forties and fifties, you may get close. The Haight's snazzy **Club Deluxe** can warp you back to 1945 the minute you walk through the doors from the sixties flashback of Haight Street. Everyone here dresses the part, with their hair as slick and shiny as their shoes (and often their sharkskin jackets). Judging by the long row of motorcycles constantly parked out front, **Cafe du Nord** is the hot spot for twentysomething cabaret hipsters. Watch for Downhear, a monthly "experimental lounge series" created to showcase the S.F. music scene's diversity, from hip-hop, psychedelia, and jazz to country, ambient house, and surf rock. Musicians and deejays take turns entertaining.

Cabaret, real not faux… The multiroom **Julie's Supper Club** and the smaller, darker **Julie Ring's Heart and Soul** have a low-key, intimate ambience; they're less scene-driven and more couples-oriented than S.F.'s popular acid jazz spots. The forties are the decade of choice at Julie Ring's. **Kimball's** is the real thing: the granddaddy of supper clubs, older and bigger (in size and in number, with offshoots in Oakland and elsewhere) than self-consciously stylized new retro nightspots. **The Coconut Grove Supper Club** is an elegantly decadent supper club with a Miami Beach feel (palm trees, pink lighting). It's pricey, but perfect for folks interested in immersing themselves in nostalgia or throwing undies at headliners like Tom Jones. As plush as its name suggests, **The Plush Room** is a cushy, cozy altogether swanky and tony cabaret room, a jewel-box setting for the likes of Rosemary Clooney, local favorite Weslia Whitfield, and other internationally known great gals. But the true jewel in the city's cabaret crown is **Harry Denton's Starlight Room**, a high-life penthouse right out of Hugh Hefner's swankier fantasies: perfect martinis, cushy couches, and grown-up glamour, all wrapped in glass, so the city sparkles like diamonds and starlight as you twirl away on the polished parquet. The Starlight Orchestra plays enjoyably cheesy Lou Rawls–type hits; lots of younger blondes show up on the arms of much older men, and cigar smoking is actually encouraged.

Drag and beyond... Despite its title, **Josie's Cabaret and Juice Joint** in the Castro is more a performance arts space than a supper club, but you can eat or drink something healthy and fruity at the front counter, then sit in a folding chair and enjoy the entertainment, which is usually healthy and fruity too. (Decorative touch we like: penile camel heads that jut semierect from one wall.) Josie's has launched several famous comedians and entertainers, including drag chameleon Lipsynka and TV sitcom casualty Margaret Cho. Fantastic drag presidential candidate and gal-about-town Joan Jett Blakk hosts a live talk show here; Da Mayor, Willie Brown himself, has been a guest. Buy your tickets in advance and get in line early; seats are not reserved and nearly all performances sell out. At **Dragstrip**, a monthly fundraising shindig, local dragstars like Elvis Herselvis, Pussy Tourette, and Justin Bond sing and entertain, while cute (hopefully) girls and boys onstage and in the audience rip off their clothes. A "dungeons and drag queens" bondage-and-domination booth is a new fixture. For real—well, almost real—glamour, try **Finocchio's**, America's most famous drag club, which has given blushing, giggling tourists something to tell the folks back home for more than half a century. Established in 1929 as a speakeasy that featured drag acts, this North Beach nightclub has presented the best cross-dressing entertainment in the city, with a revue boasting a dozen female impersonators and bawdy vaudeville jokesters. This is show biz: glitzy dresses, sculpted wigs, and more glamour than you can shake a stick at. Master of ceremonies and legendary drag performer Jose Sarria once ran for the San Francisco Board of Supervisors—before Stonewall.

And now for something completely different... For kitschy cool, nothing beats the must-see, mai-tai-fueled performances of **The Tonga Room** at the Fairmont Hotel. Sit at a table lit with flaming torches and sip a neon-hued Polynesian concoction from a tiki-head glass laden with plastic palm trees, umbrellas, and swizzle sticks, while the house band plays sincere cover tunes on a raft floating in the swimming pool "lagoon" in the center of the room. Suddenly, a tropical storm appears, complete with rain, lightning, and thunder! This is the real thing; the grass-skirted band is totally not kidding, and neither are your fellow "vacationers," who will mostly be actual middle-aged tourists who grew up listening to this music. After all those ironic, knowingly smirking hipsters at those other retro clubs, the lack of irony comes as quite a relief.

A touch of burlesque... For straight men, there are institutions of pleasure for every taste starting with the famous and well-appointed **Mitchell Brothers O'Farrell Theater**, which connoiseur Hunter S. Thompson called "the Carnegie Hall of public sex in America." It has spawned such porn stars as Marilyn Chambers in its capacious theaters. Recent performers have included Divine Brown, Hugh Grant's carmate, who reenacted the seamy auto-erotic scene (and subsequent arrest) with an all-girl cast. In North Beach, perched on Telegraph Hill just above the business district, self-consciously swanky **Centerfolds** is where upscale businessmen head for a little after-work lap dancing. The management has made some hilarious attempts at "class," including valet parking and outdoor statuary, but inside it's the same old thang. Elegant as far as strip clubs go, **The Gold Club** is perfectly positioned for conventioneers and suits, as it's sitting pretty just a block from the Moscone Center. We know where to look for you after those boring all-day seminars. **Crazy Horse** is a rowdy downtown strip club next door to the Warfield, attracting tourists and Tenderloin types with the usual array of lap dancing, wall, and VIP dancing, plus a movie room called the Sinema.

A touch of male burlesque... For men who like looking at men, the two most palatable venues are the Campus Theatre and the Nob Hill Cinema. The **Campus Theatre** is famous for its in-your-face all-male strip shows. A $12 cover fee gets you in and out all day. The theater's iffy Tenderloin location and overall shabbiness preclude snobbery, so the strippers—and the clientele—are friendly. Just a few blocks up the hill from Union Square is the all-male **Nob Hill Cinema**; with its plush carpeting, scrubbed interior, and steep ($20) admission, it attracts the discerning porn palace habitué and keeps out some of the ickier element that usually lurk in these places.

A walk on the wild side... Due to San Francisco city laws and regulations, there are no bathhouses in the city (however, both Berkeley and San Jose have bustling baths). And though AIDS still weighs heavily on everyone's minds and hearts, the free-for-all spirit of the baths still lives on in the mutated form of "sex clubs," ranging from casual, one-night-a-week affairs like "Mike's Party," in a Castro apartment, to the four-story erotic theme park called **The Playground**, which caters to many different sexual specialties every night of the week. Almost all of these clubs stress safe-sex education. The grandest of them all (or at least the cleanest) is **Eros**, which calls itself "San Francisco's Safe Sex Center." On the outside, it looks like an office building. First-timers have to buy a $5 membership (good for a year), and must read a laminated sheet with rather detailed, lengthy safe-sex guidelines. Then, before you get your membership card, you have to answer a quiz question. If you pass, you get your permit to play—just like Driver's Ed! Hand over $6 more (before 7pm; $12 after) and a buck for a towel, and you're buzzed in. Stash your clothes in lockers, put on your playclothes (or not) and explore the two-story space, which includes a roomy TV lounge; erotic murals; framed pictures of heroically (no, impossibly) proportioned men; a clean, big sauna and steam room; and upstairs, where the action is, two big playrooms, subdivided with bunk beds, slings, and other sites for scenes. At **Blow Buddies**, there are five areas, including a sweaty red-light district with a sling. They won't let you in if you're wearing cologne. **Mack**, in the heart of the club and leather district, is for the leather-minded male looking for other leather-minded males. There's a distinctly leather feel, with black walls and dim red lights, and shadowy corners. Do you deserve a good spanking? What have you done to deserve it? Bondage-a-Go-Go is a three-year-old fetish spot for goths, modern primitives, primates, and plain-looking but dirty-minded participants and voyeurs, held weekly at the **Trocadero**.

The Index

Baby Judy's Discotheque and Leisure Lounge. An every-Wednesday event at the Mission district's Casanova. The music is kitsch—retro white pop, TV themes—and the crowd on the dance floor is sexually polymorphous, mostly Gen X, and entirely eccentric.... *Tel 415/863–9328. At the Casanova, 527 Valencia St. between 16th and 17th Sts.; 16th St. BART stop; 22, 26 MUNI bus. Wednesdays 10–2.*

Bahia Cabana. Especially nuts around Carnival time, this Brazilian disco and restaurant with faux-tropical decor serves up a steamy blend of live salsa music, house and techno, and yummy eats.... *Tel 415/861–4202. 1600 Market St. at Franklin St.; Van Ness BART/MUNI Metro stop, F streetcar, 37 MUNI bus. Cover varies, usually $3.*

Bimbo's 365. A beautiful supper club in North Beach, where the live-music acts range from lounge music to jazz to literate indie rock and soul.... *Tel 415/474–0365. 1025 Columbus Ave. at Chestnut St., 41 MUNI bus.*

Blow Buddies. Virgin visitors pay an extra membership fee to enter this tribute to sexual ingenuity..... *Tel 415/863–HEAD. 933 Harrison St. between 5th and 6th Sts.; 12, 27, 42 MUNI bus.*

The Blue Lamp. One of the few places in the city where you can hear the blues, this downtown club is small, smoky, and home to a studiedly retro crowd.... *Tel 415/885–1464. 561 Geary St. between Taylor and Jones Sts.; Powell BART/MUNI Metro stop, F streetcar, 38 MUNI bus.*

Bottom of the Hill. Hip, medium-small Potrero Hill rock club with distinctive, sloping decor. Big stop for touring indie bands on the rise or stalling. There's a rec room in the back with a pool table, and the bar serves delicious, greasy sand-wiches and fries.... *Tel 415/621–4455. 1233 17th St. at Texas St., 22 MUNI bus.*

The Box. Where San Francisco comes to dance. A nearly decade-old Thursday-only event at a stripped-down, unpre-tentious SOMA warehouse. Great mix on the turntable and on the dance floor.... *715 Harrison St. between 3rd and 4th Sts.; 15, 42, 76 MUNI bus. Thursdays, 9–2:30.*

The Cafe. Upscale gays and lesbians form a line halfway down the block on weekend nights waiting to get into this glossy dance bar overlooking the heart of the Castro.... *Tel 861–4202. 2367 Market St. at Castro St.; Castro BART/MUNI Metro stop; F streetcar; 24, 37 MUNI bus.*

Cafe du Nord. A small basement club on Market Street with retro flavor, showcasing up-and-coming local jazz, rock, and spo-ken-word performers.... *Tel 415/979–6545. 2170 Market St. between Church and Sanchez Sts.; Church St. BART/ MUNI Metro stop, J Church and F streetcar, 37 MUNI bus.*

Campus Theater. Videos and dancers alternate on the main stage, and the dancers will meet you downstairs for the man-on-man version of the *Showgirls* scene.... *Tel 415/673–3384. 220 Jones St. between Turk and Eddy Sts.; Civic Center BART/MUNI Metro stop; F streetcar; 27, 31 MUNI bus.*

Centerfolds. Presents itself as a high-class joint.... *Tel 415/ 834–0661. 932 Montgomery St. at Broadway; 12, 15, 41, 83 MUNI bus.*

Chameleon Club. A dirty shoe box of a club for spoken-word Mondays and local rock bands.... *Tel 415/821–1891. 853 Valencia St. between 19th and 20th Sts.; 22, 26 MUNI bus.*

Club Deluxe. Everyone at this sassy retro hot spot in the Haight looks and acts like extras in a Russ Myer flick: ultramasculine and ultrafeminine.... *Tel 415/552–6949. 1511 Haight St. near Ashbury St.; 6, 7, 33, 43 MUNI bus.*

Club Townsend. A huge South of Market industrial space and the most thriving disco in town, Club Townsend is home of Club Universe, the big event Saturday on the dance-club circuit. Party people of all ages, races, genders, and orientations

SAN FRANCISCO ⟩ THE CLUB SCENE

come in for big-name deejay and live performances. Sunday nights you'll find S.F.'s most popular weekly gay nightspot, Pleasuredome. The rooms are big. The sound system is big. The boys who dance here have big muscles. The bar is big (and circular). The lighting is big (and it moves). The crowd? In a word, big. The parties go until 7am.... *Tel 415/974–6020. 177 Townsend St. at 3rd St.; 30, 45 MUNI bus.*

Club Universe. See **Club Townsend**.

Coconut Grove Supper Club. Blame nostalgia for the resurrection of this swanky throwback, designed for oldsters with lots of cash who want to relive their youth flinging underwear at headliners of Tom Jones's ilk.... *Tel 415/776–1616. 1415 Van Ness Ave. between Bush and Pine Sts., 42 MUNI bus.*

Crazy Horse. A rowdy Market Street strip venue that attracts tourists and Tenderloin types.... *Tel 415/771–6259. 980 Market St.; Civic Center BART/MUNI Metro stop; F streetcar; 22, 37 MUNI bus.*

DNA Lounge. A fun, funky, no-frills place to dance to rock and roll. Also books live acts....*Tel 415/626–1409. 375 11th St. at Harrison St.; 9, 12, 42 MUNI bus.*

Dragstrip. A monthly shindig at **DNA Lounge** (see above), which gathers drag artists, strippers, and other out-there performers. The audience can be scarier than the performers.... *Sundays, 9pm–3am.*

DV8. Four floors of fun in a SOMA dance club featuring industrial, funk, and house.... *Tel 415/957–1730. 540 Howard St. between 2nd and 3rd Sts.; 12, 76 MUNI bus.*

The Elbo Room. Downstairs, Mission bohemians drink and yak. Upstairs, there's a deejay and live acid jazz. A neighborhood fixture.... *Tel 415/552–7788. 647 Valencia St. between 17th and 18th Sts.; 26, 33 MUNI bus.*

Eleven. A sophisticated Italian restaurant with live jazz six nights a week.... *Tel 415/431–3337. 374 11th St. at Harrison St.; 9, 12, 42 MUNI bus.*

The End Up. Onetime headquarters of the rave scene, this South of Market after-hours dance bar is still a popular last stop on the dance circuit.... *Tel 415/487–6277. 401 6th St. at Harrison St.; 14, 27, 42 MUNI bus. Different events nightly. Cover varies, usually $4.*

Eros. This relatively posh sex club catering to gay men (or "men who have sex with men") prefers to call itself "San Francisco's Safe Sex Center." Privacy is not the point here.... *Tel 415/864–3767. 2501 Market St. between 14th St. and Duboce Ave.; Church St. BART/MUNI Metro stop; F streetcar; 37, 42 MUNI bus.*

Faster, Pussycat! A weekly club dominated by tough dykes and drunken bike messengers. Two or three female rock bands provide the stage entertainment.... *Tel 415/561–9771. At Covered Wagon Saloon, 911 Folsom St. between 5th and 6th Sts.; 12, 42 MUNI bus. Wednesdays, 9pm–2am.*

The Fillmore. We're all waiting for the Next Big Thing. Until then, this sixties rock landmark, recently refurbished, at least has a decent sound system and good views of the stage. Dining upstairs.... *Tel 415/346–6000. 1805 Geary Blvd. at Fillmore St.; 22, 38 MUNI bus.*

Finocchio's. Perhaps the most famous drag show in the known universe. Glitzy dresses, sculpted wigs—glamour.... *Tel 415/ 982–9388. 506 Broadway between Grant Ave. and Kearny St.; 15, 41 MUNI bus. Shows Wednesdays through Saturdays.*

Futura. An every-other-Saturday event set in a huge SOMA warehouse. The deejay spins Latin house for S.F.'s large and lively gay Latino population, but Latin-beat admirers of any stripe are welcome.... *Tel 415/665–6715. 174 King St. between 2nd and 3rd Sts., 42 MUNI bus. 10pm–3am.*

The Gold Club. Elegant as far as strip clubs go, and virtual one-stop shopping for randy conventioneers, as it's conveniently located just a block from Moscone Center.... *Tel 415/536–0300. 650 Howard St.; Powell Bart/MUNI Metro stop; F streetcar; 12, 30, 42, 45 MUNI bus.*

The Great American Music Hall. Music fans love seeing their favorites at this former turn-of-the-century bordello near the Tenderloin. The performers are real close, and you can run upstairs to the balcony to check for balding.... *Tel 415/ 885–0750. 359 O'Farrell St. at Polk St.; 19, 38 MUNI bus.*

Harry Denton's Starlight Room. Perfect martinis, cushy couches, a parquet dance floor, and a dazzling view from the 21st floor of the historic Sir Francis Drake Hotel. You gotta look sharp.... *Tel 415/392–7755. Sir Francis Drake Hotel, 450 Powell St. at Sutter St. (at Union Square), 21st floor.; Powell BART/MUNI Metro stop; F streetcar; Powell-Hyde and Powell-Mason cable car; 2, 3, 4, 76 MUNI bus.*

The Hotel Utah. Homey, folksy bar on the ground floor of a former SOMA hotel. Has a tiny stage for local bands.... *Tel 415/421–8308. 500 4th St. at Bryant St.; 30, 45 MUNI bus.*

Johnny Love's. Safari-themed singles bar with a restaurant and dance club.... *Tel 415/931–6053. 1500 Broadway at Polk St.; 19, 83 MUNI bus.*

Josie's Cabaret and Juice Joint. Always-sold-out Castro performance-arts space, where you get healthy food and beverages and top artists like drag performer Lypsinka and ex–sitcom star Margaret Cho.... *Tel 415/861–7933. 3583 16th St. at Market St.; Castro BART/MUNI Metro stop, F streetcar, 37 MUNI bus.*

Julie Ring's Heart and Soul. Home of the chanteuse, this intimate supper club favors standard jazz combos fronted by female vocalists.... *Tel 415/673–7100. 1695 Polk St. at Clay St.; all cable cars, 19 MUNI bus.*

Julie's Supper Club. Dark bar, bright dining room, fruity drinks. The live jazz and R&B—Thursday through Saturday—is average in this SOMA club.... *Tel 415/861–0707. 1123 Folsom St. between 7th and 8th Sts.; 12, 42 MUNI bus. Closed Sun.*

Kilowatt. Mission rock club with consistently strong bookings.... *Tel 415/861–2595. 3160 16th St. at Valencia St.; 22, 26 MUNI bus.*

Kimball's. A high-tone supper club in Hayes Valley featuring world-renowned jazz and R&B performers, both young and old. Salsa makes weekend appearances.... *Tel 415/861–5555. 300 Grove St. at Franklin St.; Van Ness BART/MUNI Metro stop; F streetcar; 21, 42, 47, 49 MUNI bus.*

Litterbox. Attitude-free fun with seventies and eighties oldies in room full of frisky queens and the occasional straight.... *No* *telephone. 683 Clementina Alley between Howard and Folsom Sts. at 8th St.; 12, 27, 76 MUNI bus. Fridays.*

Mack. Yes, there are still leather men, and this is where they go to find others.... *Tel 415/558–8300. 317 10th St. between Folsom and Harrison Sts.; Van Ness BART/MUNI Metro stop; F streetcar; 12, 42 MUNI bus.*

Miss Pearl's Jam House. A rock-star hangout, perhaps because it's attached to the Phoenix Hotel, where many bands stay during S.F. tour stops. The food (jerked chicken and other spicy meats) and the music (often reggae) are Caribbean. Large dance floor.... *Tel 415/775–5267. 601 Eddy St. between Polk and Larkin Sts.; 19, 31 MUNI bus.*

Mitchell Brothers O'Farrell Theatre. Maybe the world's most famous and handsomely appointed strip club.... *Tel 415/ 776–6686. Polk and O'Farrell Sts.; 19, 42, 47, 49 MUNI bus.*

New Wave City. Floating, monthly party paying tribute to that not-so-distant past when Flock of Seagulls and the Go-Gos were pop forces to be reckoned with.... *Tel 415/675–LOVE. Address changes each month. Saturday, 9–3.*

Nickie's BBQ. A long, narrow hole-in-the-wall with lots of charm. Famous (at least in S.F.) deejay Cheb I. Sabbah spins world music every Tuesday at this Lower Haight site. The Tuesday crowd is as international as the music. Be warned: Mondays are Grateful Dead fests.... *Tel 415/621– 6508. 460 Haight St. at Filmore St.; 6, 7, 43 MUNI bus.*

Nightbreak. A small rocker dive, with a small stage in one corner. One of the few remaining refuges for big-hair bands in S.F., though most bills here are punk.... *Tel 415/221–9008. 1821 Haight St. near Stanyan St.; 6, 7, 43 MUNI bus.*

Nob Hill Cinema. In addition to movies, it has live shows featuring name-brand porn stars and a startlingly pristine peep arcade.... *Tel 415/781–9468. 729 Bush St. between Powell and Mason Sts.; all streetcars, 30 MUNI bus.*

Paradise Lounge. If there's a rock-and-roll heaven, it looks something like this SOMA club, which has three stages running simultaneously.... *Tel 415/861–6906. 1501 Folsom St. at 11th St.; 12, 42 MUNI bus.*

The Pit. A bar that hosts the dregs of the weekend, beginning at 5am Monday mornings, with a club called Rehab.... *No telephone. 9th St. at Howard St.; Civic Center BART/MUNI Metro stop; F streetcar; 12, 19, 42 MUNI bus.*

Plastik. Thursday night gathering for male and female super-models and wannabes. The music: fashionable house and techno.... *Tel 415/777–0666. At Big Heart City, 836 Mission St. between 4th and 5th Sts.; 15, 26 MUNI bus. 9pm–3am.*

The Playground. San Francisco's newest and largest sex club, with all flavors of sex play on four levels.... *Tel 415/864–PLAY. 74 Otis St. between S. Van Ness Ave. and Gough St.; Van Ness BART/MUNI Metro stop; F streetcar; 14, 49 MUNI bus.*

Pleasuredome. See **Club Townsend**.

The Plush Room. Sumptuous cabaret room attracting the best singers in the business and a très chic crowd... *Tel 415/885–2800. In the York Hotel, 940 Sutter St. between Leavenworth and Hyde Sts.; 2, 3, 4, 30, 45 MUNI bus.*

The Purple Onion. Ground zero of the local surf-rock revival. This North Beach bar, a Beat-era hot spot, has a frat-party, boys-clubhouse atmosphere complete with kegs.... *Tel 415/398–8415. 140 Columbus Ave. at Montgomery St.; 15, 41 MUNI bus.*

The Saloon. Rowdy, "atmospheric," and always packed, this legendary North Beach joint is one of the best spots in the city for jazz and blues, or just to hide out.... *Tel 415/397–3751. 1232 Grant Ave. at Green St.; 15, 41 MUNI bus.*

Slim's. Boz Scaggs' midsized rock venue, mostly for modern-rock radio and neo-psychedelia. Youngsters, yuppies, and music-biz types are frequent fixtures. Expensive.... *Tel 415/522–0333. 333 11th St. between Folsom and Harrison Sts.; 12, 42 MUNI bus.*

Sound Factory. Multilevel discotheque producing house, tech-no, and funk for the masses. Dress code: No sneakers, hooded sweats, or baseball caps.... *Tel 415/543–1300. 525 Harrison St. at 1st St., 42 MUNI bus. Cover varies, usually $10. 9pm–7am.*

The Stud. A popular gay and lesbian dance bar for more than 25 years. Its cozy, woody decor and friendly staff draw all sorts of folks keen on letting their hair down.... *Tel 415/242–STUD. 399 9th St. at Harrison St., 42 MUNI bus. Cover varies, usually $3.*

330 Ritch. Industrial-chic supper club hidden in a small SOMA alley. Hip-hop on weekdays, acid jazz on weekends, always beautiful people.... *Tel 415/522–9558. 330 Ritch St., in Ritch Alley between 3rd and 4th Sts. off Townsend St.; 12, 76 MUNI bus.*

The Tonga Room. Faux-Polynesian cocktail lounge at the Fairmont Hotel, where a grass-skirted band plays in the middle of an indoor lagoon between simulated thunderstorms. Unique.... *Tel 415/772–5000. Basement of the Fairmont Hotel, 950 Mason St. at California St.; Powell-Mason cable car, 30 MUNI bus.*

Trocadero. Huge two-floor club South of Market, once a gay mecca, now young and punk. Our favorite night is Wednesday, when Bondage-a-Go-Go brings out the suburban leather enthusiasts.... *Tel 415/495–6620. 520 4th St. at Bryant St.; 12, 76 MUNI bus.*

Up & Down Club. Downstairs, there's live music by local young jazz acts; upstairs, there's dancing to deejay selections. Supermodel Christy Turlington is a co-owner.... *Tel 415/626–2388. 1151 Folsom St. at 7th St., 12 MUNI bus.*

V/SF. Finally, dancing but no smoking. On most nights, the crowd at this clean, classy, and pricey club is mostly gay. G-Spot, the all-girl night, has settled here Saturdays from 8pm to 2am.... *Tel 415/621–1530. 278 11th St. at Folsom St.; 9, 12, 42 MUNI bus. Cover varies, usually $10.*

The Warfield. S.F.'s largest rock venue, this former movie palace is, of course, the crown jewel of Bill Graham's music empire. Drawbacks: The staff can be rude, and the standing area at the front of the stage is tiny.... *Tel 415/775–7722. 962 Market St. at Taylor St.; Civic Center BART/MUNI Metro stop, F streetcar, 37 MUNI bus.*

San Francisco Clubs

Bahia Cabana	**1**		The End Up	**12**
Bimbo's 365	**2**		Faster, Pussycat!	**13**
The Blue Lamp	**3**		The Fillmore	**14**
The Box	**4**		Finocchio's	**15**
The Cafe	**5**		Futura	**16**
Club Townsend	**6**		The Great American Music Hall	**17**
Coconut Grove Supper Club	**7**		Harry Denton's Starlight Room	**19**
DNA Lounge	**8**		The Hotel Utah	**20**
DV8	**10**		Johnny Love's	**21**
Eleven	**11**		Julie Ring's Heart and Soul	**22**

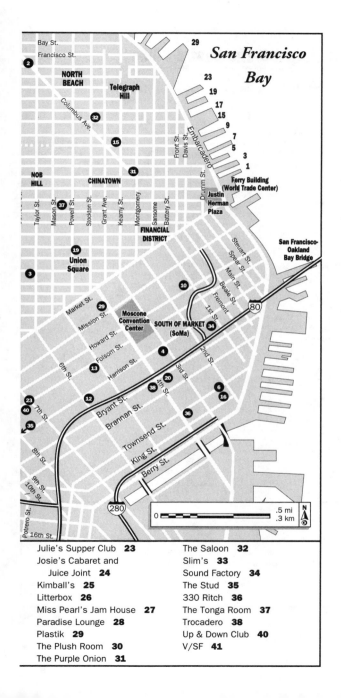

San Francisco Bay

NORTH BEACH

Telegraph Hill

Columbus Ave.

NOB HILL

CHINATOWN

Taylor St.
Mason St.
Powell St.
Stockton St.
Grant Ave.
Kearny St.
Montgomery
Sansome St.
Battery St.

Front St.
Davis St.
Embarcadero
Drumm St.

Ferry Building (World Trade Center)

Justin Herman Plaza

FINANCIAL DISTRICT

Union Square

San Francisco-Oakland Bay Bridge

Market St.

Mission St.

Moscone Convention Center

SOUTH OF MARKET (SoMa)

Howard St.
Folsom St.
Harrison St.

6th St.

Bryant St.
Brannan St.

Townsend St.

King St.

Berry St.

8th St.
9th St.
10th St.
Potrero St.
16th St.

Steuart St.
Spear St.
Main St.
Beale St.
Fremont
1st St.
2nd St.
3rd St.
4th St.

280

80

0   .5 mi
     .3 km

N

The Haight & The Castro Clubs

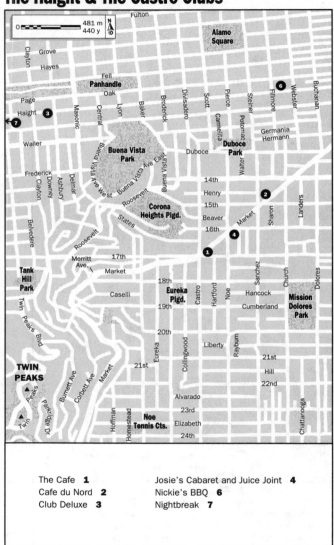

The Cafe **1**

Cafe du Nord **2**

Club Deluxe **3**

Josie's Cabaret and Juice Joint **4**

Nickie's BBQ **6**

Nightbreak **7**

Mission District Clubs

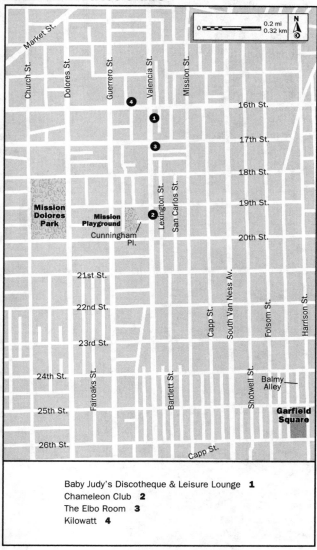

Baby Judy's Discotheque & Leisure Lounge **1**
Chameleon Club **2**
The Elbo Room **3**
Kilowatt **4**

the bar

scene 2

Even in San Francisco, a town where fun is an industry, people have a difficult time associating bars with heightened intelligence. The beatniks had bennies; hippies had electric Kool-Aid acid tests; and the rave kids of the late eighties had smart drinks. Thankfully the smart drinks, like the rest, came and went. But as a mood enhancer of choice, booze will never disappear from San Francisco. Whether it's a gallon jug of burgundy with an acoustic guitar or high-balls and goatees, this town likes a good drink—against a good backdrop.

The Anchor Steam company continues to bottle the same type of steam beer that 19th-century gold prospectors once spent their nuggets on (at a brewery in continuous operation since 1886, actually), and it's available in almost every bar in town. In 1952, Irish coffee was first introduced to the states at San Francisco's Buena Vista Cafe on the Wharf. The world has San Francisco to thank for the gin martini. And one 1970s Financial District bar featured go-go movies at eye level above the men's-room urinals. Jerry Garcia may have passed on, but the Grateful Dead now has a microbrew named in its honor—just don't lick the label. The newest variations on the bar theme seem to be microbrewed beer, a martini comeback, and smoking, a healthy—or unhealthy—backlash to a perceived California health obsession. Jogging is out, gin is in.

However you categorize them, most San Francisco bars emulate the mood of an old-fashioned saloon, offering atmosphere created by gregarious townsfolk along with the occasional out-of-town stranger who strolls through the swinging doors. One such place, Izzy's Saloon (which has re-opened as a steakhouse), was actually the inspiration for William Saroyan's Pulitzer prize–winning play, *The Time of Your Life*. In a typical San Francisco maneuver, he refused the award.

Etiquette
Slip your bartender or waitress at least a buck for every drink. It's good manners, they'll appreciate it, and you'll get good service. If your sole interest is to save money, stay home and drink on the sofa.

Getting Around
Drinkers' caveat: You can easily find yourself encountering a police sobriety-test roadblock set up on a city street, especially on holidays. If the officer acts suspicious in any way, tell him you're going straight home. In California, drunk driving carries the same stigma as shooting up a schoolyard, so if you're thinking of getting a little heat on, take a taxi or the MUNI transit system, which costs a dollar for three stops.

The Lowdown

The lone pool table (dives, part 1)... San Francisco is no stranger to billiards, the city's pool halls finding themselves in both the recent book *Playing Off the Rail: A Pool Hustler's Journey* by David McCumber, and the Rob Nilsson film *Chalk*. But another pool setting has gone unnoticed: the dive bar with only one table. Pool isn't really the point of the visit, but if you've got a hankering for competition and hand-eye coordination, there's usually a banged-up table in the back room that will take your quarters. The **Zeitgeist** on Valencia in the Mission district can't be missed—just look for the line of European motorcycles parked out front. Or it might be their logo that stands out, a mutation of a human skull and the Playboy bunny silhouette. The beer list is extensive, video monitors are tuned to the sports channel—especially if there's bike or Formula One car racing on—and the outdoor patio is the perfect place to sit in the sun, try one of their sandwiches, and watch bikers do cartwheels (literally). For a more competitive pool game, the **Armadillo's** in the Lower Haight provides Wild West decor and loud, loud Rolling Stones. Choose from several beers on tap, and don't mind the herd of neighborhood dogs wandering around, bumping into your legs. If they all start barking at once, you know you've come on a good night. The **500 Club** on Guerrero tucks its table in an adjacent room, and the goatee/bowling-shirt crowd either bellies up to the bar or slinks into the heavy vinyl booths. Free hors d'oeuvres on Fridays, and drink specials change every day. One block away on 16th Street is **Doctor Bombay's,** a vaguely sinister emporium with dark wooden booths that remind you of a Swiss chalet. To prime themselves for the pool table in the back room, the foolhardy turn to the Jagermeister on tap.

More microbrews, please... It seems you can't walk into a bar anymore without gazing upon an army of beer taps in various shapes, from a Golden Gate Bridge arch to bears, apples, pears, and proud family crests. Whether you wear a suit or Doc Martens, you now live in a micro-brew age of unlimited opportunity; and if you haven't sampled every Boont Amber Triple-Filtered Cider Bock Stout there is, apparently you must be some kind of wimp (and can't make new friends, either). If you like your beer in at least 61 flavors, you deserve a stop at any of the **Jack's** scattered throughout the city's neighborhoods. The Fillmore one is the original location, a blues joint open since 1932, and is also reportedly the oldest operating music club west of the Mississippi, featuring wall photos of John Lee Hooker and Joe Louis. Formerly in the heart of the city's black district, it now features lots of Gap kids from the condos down the block, and the historic Fill-more concert hall just across the street. For more of a Lower Haight, grunge-goatee, tie-your-dog-to-a-parking-meter atmosphere, the beer flows freely at the **Toronado**—a wall lists a staggering 45 different vari-eties—and occasional cigar nights are also held here. Across the street can be found a good selection of British beers and ales at the **Mad Dog in the Fog**—similar crowd but with a penchant for darts. Pub grub begins in the morning, and after a plate of bangers and mash, the day begins. The **Lucky 13** boasts 30 beers, including those German ones with decorative tap pulls standing 2 feet tall. Twenty-something night owls pack the long, narrow space, which is decorated with old exploitation-movie posters, all featuring the number 13.

Faded sports bars... San Francisco is unique in that we keep building ballparks, tearing them down, building new ones, and arguing about it all the while. But what is left in the rubble of yesteryear's playing fields are the neighborhood sports bars that once fueled the fans. The San Francisco Seals baseball stadium in the Potrero dis-trict was torn down years ago to make a parking lot, but across the street remains the **Double Play**, a classic politico stop for a drink and a sit-down lunch. Check out the vintage baseball mitts on the walls. The historic Kezar Stadium next to Golden Gate Park, once home to 49er games as well as Dirty Harry movies, has recently been remodeled and reopened for local school athletics; across the street the **Kezar Club** still keeps the neighborhood quenched. Look for the ceiling covered with sports jerseys, posters, and pennants, and the seriously competitive games of pool on the twin tables in the back room. After a long career as both player and manager of the San Francisco Seals, Frank J. "Lefty" O'Doul opened a joint of his own in 1958. **Lefty O'Doul's** piano bar and restaurant caters to both Union Square tourists and hearing-aid old-timers who remember the good old days. Chefs will still slice you up a roast beef platter, and you can watch old folks sing "Misty" or examine the walls filled with photos of Joe DiMaggio, the legend whom O'Doul helped develop.

Must-sees for first-time visitors from Peoria...

Although they may not want to admit it, locals depend heavily upon the free-spending habits of the genus *la turista muy dinero*. At the **Buena Vista Cafe**, you'll find mostly out-of-staters shivering in their shorts, thinking they're in the warm part of California. It overlooks the bay near Fisherman's Wharf, and in addition to having a full kitchen was the first place in the country to serve Irish coffee. The popular Bay Area drink was introduced to America in 1952 by newspaper columnist Stanton Delaplane. Another popular habitat for *la turista* is Union Square. Sandwiched between department stores and discount electronics shops, the gaudy **Gold Dust** has poured highballs since 1933 and features live Dixieland jazz seven nights a week. Settle into one of the high-backed booths and tap your toe to a trombone solo as naked women cavort over your head in an ancient ceiling mural. Tourists also frequent the Italian North Beach neighborhood, once home to Barbary Coast opium dens and whorehouses, and later, Kerouac and the rest of the Beat poets. The **Saloon** on Grant is one of the oldest bars in the city, saved from the 1906 earthquake fire by a bucket brigade of panicked patrons. Today it showcases cheap drinks and nightly blues bands. Keep an eye on your drink, because the harmonica player just may start dancing on top of the bar. Down one block is Spec's, or, technically, **Spec's 12 Adler Museum Cafe**, founded by a merchant seaman who stuffed the place full of eccentric treasures from his travels abroad. Locals read the paper during the day; in the evening,

SAN FRANCISCO ⟨ THE BAR SCENE

expect everyone from weathered old poets to tables of birthday parties. Across the street and next to City Lights Bookstore is **Vesuvio**, its atmosphere little different from the Beat poetry days. Local regulars include the Jefferson Airplane's Paul Kantner, and the upstairs seating offers a great view of the street over a pitcher of Anchor Steam. Gay tourists are flocking to **Harvey's** in the Castro. Formerly known as the Elephant Walk, Harvey's gained notoriety during the 1978 citywide riots following the assassination of gay city supervisor Harvey Milk. Gay memorabilia now gives it a cheesy Hard Rock spin: one of Liberace's sequined jackets, Speedo swim trunks of Greg Louganis's, a racquet from Martina Navratilova, and a nun's habit from Sister Boom Boom of the drag-nun group Sisters of Perpetual Indulgence.

Look mom, we're retro!... Like it or not, America is caught in the throes of a retro-cocktail revolution, from clothes and music and graphic design to a renewed affinity for the olive. If alcohol and nicotine are being marginalized by our increased health awareness, then by all means let's go back to an era where we can pollute ourselves without guilt. After years of being boarded up, the former old-school spaghetti supper club known as **Bruno's** has recently reopened at the same location with a complete interior overhaul. One of the newest spots for the Mission crowd who prefer chain-smoking in nice sports coats, the kitchen offers a menu that changes nightly, and the booths are of the finest virgin vinyl. Martinis are the specialty at the **Club Deluxe** in the Upper Haight, a black-and-polished-aluminum den of cocktail carnage, where budding Sinatras share the stage with jazz and swing bands. Retro swing jazz is also industry standard for the **Cafe du Nord**, but prepare to pay a nominal cover charge. The retro crowd has moved off South of Market's **Julie's Supper Club** for better pastures such as the above, but Julie's was one of the first, and still hires the best bartenders in town. True retros now avoid it, leaving room for the retro bridge-and-tunnel crowd from across the bay. (See The Club Scene for Club Deluxe, Cafe du Nord, and Julie's Supper Club.)

Always were retro... Tiki bars once thrived in California after World War II, when returning G.I.'s brought the island culture back home with them. Sadly, although San Francisco is still a port town, there are few left. But the survivors carry on, and a new generation of young rumrunners seems to be keeping the tiki torch lit. **Trad'r Sam** is conveniently located way, way the hell out on Geary toward the ocean, but if you're not a designated driver, it's well worth the visit. When S.F.'s nouveau mods line their mopeds up out front, it feels like *Quadrophenia*-meets-*Blue Hawaii*. All the furniture is made of wrapped cane, and every booth is named for a different group of South Seas islands. Enjoy a hideously strong rum punch concoction while sitting in Guam or Hawaii. For something more formal, the **Tonga Room** at the Fairmont Hotel atop Nob Hill offers not just full-throttle tropical decorations and waiter costumes, but also a live band floating in a tiny boat in the swimming pool. (See The Club Scene.)

Quittin' time... Like Fred Flintstone sliding down the dinosaur's neck on bird-call cue or the old ad slogan, "It's Miller Time," the end of the workday often means it's time to go soak your head in a bowl of whatever suits your taste. If you're a daily commuter shuttling home through the downtown Transbay Terminal, you'll probably belly up to **Cuddles** for some transportation fortification before hopping that train or bus. Settle into some groovy white vinyl furniture, ignore the grubby dude with the backpack, and look out the windows at the newsstand and the Highway Patrol office across the lobby. When the final whistle blows for local politicos, they head for the **Washington Square Bar & Grill** in North Beach, where power brokers can cut into a plate of veal, listen to live jazz, and ponder the city's next move. When the stage lights go dark, many actors and other members of the theater community head for the **Rite Spot** in the Potrero district, where the evening's show is dissected again and again over the candlelit tablecloths, while an out-of-tune house piano is put to good use. Every Friday spells relief for the city's bicycle messengers, who congregate and wheel their bikes into the **Covered Wagon** South of Market, a noisy, graffiti-splashed dive that pours equal parts beer and Jagermeister. If it isn't a live band playing Jimi Hendrix cover tunes, it's the sound system playing Jimi Hendrix CDs. The **Slow Club** in the Potrero serves espresso and lunch during the day, but at night the industrial furniture fills up with staffers from the nearby *Bay Guardian* weekly newspaper and KQED, the city's public radio/television station conglomerate. Depending on the intensity of the *Guardian*'s weekly sniping at KQED's funding and policies, they may even sit on the same side of the room. (See Late Night Dining.)

Where the literati roam... Where you find bars, you'll find writers, and in a town with so much literary tradition, you never know who you'll bump into. Is it the next Kerouac or Dashiell Hammett? **Gino & Carlo** in North Beach seems to attract them like flies—or, more accurately, barflies. Legendary local sportswriter and syndicated columnist Charles McCabe used to write his daily *Chronicle* column here every morning, fueled by six Rainier ales. He is now gone, but his portrait hangs framed above the bar. The regulars are either ruddy-faced locals, or cunning young pool sharks working the tables in the back room. Most of the current *Chronicle* staff, and those from the rival afternoon *Examiner*, can be found at the **M & M**, a traditional newspaper bar and grill a block from both papers downtown, serving beer and burgers and way too much gossip. Linger around a conversation between reporters, and you'll know more about the town than you really care to. In the 1960s, Jerry's sports bar was the unofficial satellite office for the fledgling *Rolling Stone* magazine across the street South of Market, racking up tabs for the likes of Hunter S. Thompson and Joe Eszterhas. Now named **Zeke's**, it still does the same for the neighboring *S.F. Weekly* newspaper and *Wired* magazine. Those writers with a thirst for danger frequent the Tenderloin's **21 Club**, where the bartender will eagerly regale you with stories about the days of Hunter S. Thompson and his former-editor David McCumber. Regulars here have that look that says they probably leave only to change clothes. Hang around long enough, they'll probably buy you a round.

Dive! dive! (dives, part 2)... We've all known the quiet ecstasy of a bar that has failed to create atmosphere for so many years it actually ends up being one of the cooler places to hang out. Despite their thorough lack of attention to setting a mood, the following places are becoming more popular to a younger clientele, especially when nobody's interested in dressing up to get down. Bring your own crowd. The **Expansion** on Market Street offers little more than pinball machines, a pool table, and dust-covered model-train engines for getting in the way of drinking. The bartenders are all over 60, as are most of the patrons, who demand their Budweiser in those tiny little glasses. Prices are cheap, the jukebox has everything from soup to nuts (at respectable volume), and most of the Formica tables wobble on cue. Another such subterranean haunt in the Financial District is the **7-11 Club**, a sunken rectangle of relentless nothingness that beckons somebody, anybody, to come save it from its own misery. It might seem depressing, but many nights the place is packed with downtowners blowing off steam. Located across the street from the post office (which remains closed for seismic reinforcement), **Lloyd's** offers a reinforcement special of its own—a shot and a glass of beer for $1.50. With its peeling paint and fleabag corner location, you can't miss Lloyd's. Be warned: It's a block from one of the worst crime zones in the city.

Shaken, not stirred... The origin of the modern martini (gin, of course) dates back to at least 1867, when a recipe by Professor Jerry Thomas, a bartender at San Francisco's Occidental Hotel, first appeared in print. His initial version—gin, vermouth, and a maraschino cherry—has survived with minor modifications in bars across the world, but nowhere is it taken as seriously as at the **Occidental Grill** in the Financial District, so named in homage to the original hotel. Tending shop beneath a portrait of Jerry pouring a "Blue Blazer," one Occidental bartender will pour an estimated 75 martinis on your average working day. Their procedure is classic—ice is briefly coated with vermouth, then drained, and shaken with gin until the shaker accumulates a thin coating of frost. The results are strained into a glass and garnished with your choice—all done tableside if so desired. The bar also offers two humidors of cigars, selling 300 to 400 a week, with periodic private cigar evenings to separate the boys from the men. As the sign above the door announces, "Smoking prohibited except in designated areas such as the bar, where we invite you to enjoy a cigar without fear of imprisonment or public stoning." South of Market's **Cafe**

Mars specializes in a Martian martini, made with cranberry Finlandia. The postindustrial interior makes a great place to plug in a Powerbook; it's in an area inhabited by upstart design firms, *Wired*, HTML entrepreneurs, and other Internet geeks. Martinis at the **Club Deluxe** in the Upper Haight feature vermouth sprayed into the glass from a mister, followed by shaken gin or vodka. Don't even think of ordering a vodka martini at the **Persian Aub Zam Zam** down the street. Bartender Bruno has no compunction about suddenly kicking out people he doesn't like, including the novices who order vodka instead of gin. If you enjoy intimidation, dress nicely, shut up, and look in amazement at all the empty tables.

League of nations... Since the United Nations was founded in the city in 1945, it seems appropriate that there would be a variety of cultures represented in the panorama of bars. The **Li Po** bar has been an institution in the heart of Chinatown since at least 1928—the bartender isn't exactly sure. Underneath a 6-foot-tall hanging lamp and statue shrine, you can order Chinese rice whiskey, or try the Li Po Special, a snifter with seven shots of booze, for an economical $5.50. It's a favorite secret haunt of North Beach hipsters who don't want to attract attention, preferring to hide out on the upstairs sofas. Walls are decorated with currency from all over the world, and to complete the culture clash, the Beatles' "Lady Madonna" plays on the sound system. The **Edinburgh Castle** on Geary opens up into a beautiful two-story pub with thick wooden tables, darts, and pool. If the big caber bolted to the wall isn't a tip-off you're in Scottish territory, the assortment of single-malt scotches will be. Waiters will take your order, run around the corner, and bring back steaming fish and chips wrapped in the morning's paper, and entertainment may range from a bagpiper to a bluegrass band. One night the bartender came out from behind the plank and read everyone a poem about venereal disease. Hopping one island over to Ireland, Irish pride runs strong in San Francisco neighborhoods and politics, and especially at **Ireland's 32**, where IRA posters and portraits of people like James Joyce fight for space on the walls and ceiling. You don't have to be Irish to stay, but ordering a Brit beer, such as Bass ale, is definitely in poor taste. The large S.F. Spanish-speaking population is well represented at **La Rondalla**, a crowded Mission bar and restaurant where people from all backgrounds wrestle for space amidst margaritas and live mariachi music.

Caucasian hormones gone mad... Since at least the sixties, a Marina district intersection known as The Triangle has been ground zero for the white singles scene. Nobody knows why it coalesces at this spot, nor does anybody really care. If you don't live in the Marina, you don't set foot here. On one corner of Fillmore and Greenwich, there's the **City Tavern**, where, beyond the picture windows, beveled-glass doors, dark wood, and brass accents, lies a bevy of good-looking, pedigreed young people in expensive pressed jeans. The full restaurant with tablecloths provides a good place to sit down with someone for an outside-of-work cocktail. Across the intersection from the City Tavern is the **Balboa Cafe**, where, beyond the picture windows, beveled glass doors, dark wood, and brass accents, lies a bevy of good-looking, pedigreed young people in expensive pressed jeans. The full restaurant with tablecloths provides a good place to loosen the tie and—you get the idea. The **Pierce Street Annex** sits, well, not quite on the third corner, but almost, and since 1962 has catered to a more down-to-earth crowd. No pressed jeans, but the hormones are still turned up full blast. Big video screens alert you to the sports theme at work here, which means it's perfectly acceptable to get drunk and wear school sweatshirts. Two blocks up Fillmore at Union Street, the **Tarr & Feathers** caters to young Gap-heads stewing in their own excitement, desirous of some live music with their microbrews. The picture windows proudly announce that Tarr & Feathers is the first bar in San Francisco to serve Jagermeister on tap! Dude! Another favorite Caucasian meeting place is **Johnny Love's** at Broadway and Polk, for years a ferny singles bar. This version carries on the tradition, with a noisy mixture of stewardesses—er, flight attendants—football players, and those privileged enough to be near them. The regular reggae and blues bands serenade the line of hair-gelled hopefuls outside the picture windows, waiting for validation from the doorman.

See-and-be-scenes... Historically, these establishments are what put San Francisco on the map for out-of-towners. They're sets for movies, hangouts for movie stars, window dressing for brochures. But, most importantly to locals, we can enjoy them without feeling like we're constantly elbowing with tourists. The most famous North Beach outdoor bar and cafe is **Enrico's**, opened years ago by Enrico Banducci, whose nightclub ventures helped launch the careers of Barbra Streisand, Bill Cosby, Woody Allen, and Phyllis Diller. After a lengthy closing, the original Enrico's is again open under new ownership, featuring outdoor eating (with newly installed heaters for those cold S.F. nights; i.e., every one), and live jazz. Grab one of the many seats with a great view, watch the parade walk past, and pretend you're the new breed of Beat poet, composing free verse on your laptop. Around the corner from Enrico's on Columbus is **Tosca**, an old Italian institution done in red vinyl. High-profile book-release parties are often held here. Celebrities from Sam Shepard to Francis Ford Coppola have taken advantage of the secret invitation-only pool room in the rear. (See The Cafe Scene.)

Comes with the view... After successfully opening white-collar bars named after himself, including Harry's and Harry Denton's, and training another entrepreneur who also named a white-collar bar after himself (Johnny Love), Mr. Denton recently turned his sights to revamping the old sky-view bar on top of the Sir Francis Drake Hotel at Union Square. The refurbished, upscale **Harry Denton's Starlight Room** offers one of the newest coat-and-tie views of the entire city, and is a magnet for socialites as well as hotel guests. For the purest gaze on the Pacific, the **Ben Butler Bar** in the Cliff House teeters on the edge of the United States, where Geary runs into the sea. Adjacent to the Cliff House are the ruins of an early-20th-century public bathhouse which burned down in a fire many years ago. Fun for a quick, if dangerous, hike. The parking spaces are filled with tour buses, but if you settle down into an antique sofa in the bar and look out at the waves crashing against the rocks, your mind will wander from the tourists and mediocre food to more philosophical musings like, "How many years have the birds pooped on those rocks, anyway?" If a view of the bay is more your cup of grog, it's hard to beat the low-key San Francisco waterfront feel of **Pier 23**, where the bar as well as the outdoor tables all face the water. The seafood is excellent here, and you can watch the ships roll in, just like Otis Redding did. You can also watch the seagulls land on your table and scare the kids, which is entertainment that just can't be bought. Afternoons are best for a quiet cocktail; the place is packed nights with dining and live music. The Mission dive known as **El Rio** technically has no view of the water, but its huge backyard patio is a view unto itself, ideal for lounging in a faux tropical setting. Imagine your own scenic vista, without the hassle of an ocean breeze to throw you off your game. The crowd is mixed, straight and gay, and most nights are dedicated to either dancing or live bands. At least stop by for the matchbooks, which boast, "Your Dive."

If you build it, they will come (gimmick bars)...

One of the hottest new spots in the city is crowded even on weeknights, for a few reasons. First, the **Red Room** is adjacent to the renovated Commodore Hotel; it catches a spillover of trendy clientele from comedians to rock bands. But more important, people come here because the Red Room is red. Completely red, as in walls, ceiling, furniture, lighting. Cocktails are preferred over beer, so bring your goatee and smoke 'em if you got 'em. This place is so much of a scene, you expect a fashion shoot in progress for *Details* magazine, with bored-looking young girls modeling some kind of silver midriff-exposing space suits. Martinis are poured huge but heavy on the vermouth, and the bartenders are appropriately aloof, especially if you're not quite cool enough to be there. Computer nerds are the primary target of the brain trust behind the **Icon Byte Bar & Grill** South of Market. The walls and tables are covered with all kinds of computer circuit boards, old monitors, junk from decades of rapidly outdated technology. Of course, true computer geeks rarely leave their homes, but if they did visit here, they'd most likely log onto the Internet at the terminal provided, and continue geeking. A frequent location for computer industry–related parties and receptions, Icon offers lunch and dinner menus, as well as a full bar and several beers on tap. But the most peculiar gimmick bar in the city began completely by accident years ago, when the wife of the owner decided to fill up an empty wall with pictures of clowns. Today, the **Embers** in the Sunset district is jammed with hundreds of clowns of all persuasions—Harlequins, Pantaloons, Scaramouches, Emmett Kellys, creepy Czech marionettes—donated by customers from all over the world. Owner Jack Bouey has run the joint since it opened in 1955, and is the first to admit that none of the clowns are very valuable, because "nicotine ruins everything." One glance up at the tobacco-friendly ceiling will tell you it's okay to light up without somebody calling in the ATF bureau. Old-timer regulars open up the place each morning, but surprisingly, the weekends are filled with a young crowd who prefer the bizarre clown surroundings and lax smoking policy. Perhaps one day they'll bring back the famed Embers slogan: "If you can't get laid in the Embers, you can't get laid at all."

Hotel chic... Occasionally the urge may arise to imbibe in that most sacred of chambers, the hushed hotel annex bar. Either you're old enough to afford such luxury, and accustomed to expensing rounds of drinks in well-furnished surroundings, or you're a youngster, squandering hard-earned funds to approximate some form of what you consider adulthood. Aside from being the hotel where President Warren Harding breathed his last, the Palace features one of the largest surviving Maxfield Parrish paintings, an enormous mural that runs the length of the **Pied Piper** bar. It's worth a stop just for the sight alone. (And after tee martoonis, you can stroll next door to gawk at the big-eyed waif paintings in the Keane Eyes Gallery—see Hanging Out.) Another beautiful old hotel bar is the **Redwood Room**, tucked in the back of the Clift Hotel on Union Square, whose old-growth walls rise two stories high. Here, it is said, men were kicked off the premises back in the seventies if their hair was deemed too long. You can, no doubt, have hair over the collar these days, but it still might be a good idea not to tromp in with a backpack, mumbling about the Grateful Dead.

So much beer, so little time... Can we say it, all together? There are now enough brands of beer in the United States. No? Not yet? Not as long as there are still bars that brew their own house recipes. Founded just a few years ago, the **Gordon Biersch Brewery** has already outgrown the city enough to open up franchises throughout California and Hawaii, but here you can still visit the flagship of the fleet. Located on the Embarcadero, just a pint glass's throw away from the Gap offices and the rest of new corporate San Francisco, this has grown into a downtown black-wearing pickup joint of sorts, with a crowd regularly spilling out onto the front steps. Picture windows offer a great view of the bay, and the owners regularly feature four beers on tap. The **Twenty Tank Brewery** is conveniently located in the middle of SOMA music clubs on 11th Street off Folsom, for that pre- or postshow boost from any of six flavors, be it light lager or dark stout. Check the board above the bar; their specials change frequently. Twenty Tank also serves a sandwich-and-nachos menu, and the upstairs seating offers privacy. One drawback: High ceilings make the acoustics resemble those of an aircraft hangar. Oldest of them all is the **San Francisco Brewing Company**, allegedly once a speakeasy in North Beach. The dark wood and ceiling fans suggest a history far wilder than what goes on today, although the weekends get lively with live jazz and comedy shows. The kitchen provides sandwiches and light entrees to soak up your samples of the Emperor Norton Ale, named for San Francisco's original crazy homeless person.

Best tequilas... Hands down, the widest selection of tequilas in town is at **Tommy's Mexican Restaurant**, way the hell down Geary toward the ocean. It's a bit of a hike, but if you like tequila, the trip is well worth it. The owner is so serious about his tequila bar he makes several trips a year to Mexico, lugging back obscure labels you've never heard of, including several varieties of *reposado* (made from 100 percent agave squeezings, as opposed to most tequila, which is blended). If you crave a margarita, Tommy's makes them only with the juice of real limes. Another excellent margarita is prepared by the **Occidental Grill**. Their house spicy margaritas are made by marinating white tequila in jars of peppers, which the bartender will gladly show you upon request.

For the boys... San Francisco's first gay bar, The Dash, closed in 1908, but the **Twin Peaks** ranks among the oldest surviving saloons specializing in men. It was the first gay bar in the country to actually install picture windows, at the time a dangerous decision. The beautiful corner structure is laid-back and comfortable, even though the predominately older clientele have given it bitchy nicknames, like "the Glass Coffin" or "God's Waiting Room."

Financial District gays who like a downscale environment stop by **Ginger's Trois**, a gaudy hole-in-the-wall where Christmas lights blink year-round and patrons are frequently found singing along with Dion's "Runaway" on the jukebox. If you want full-fledged karaoke, **The Mint** offers seven nights a week of it. Always a noisy time, and if all that harmony makes you hungry, the Hot N Chunky hamburger joint is right next door. Asian gays congregate at the **N Touch** on Polk Street, which features videos and a small dance floor. The leather scene is much less visible than in the pre-AIDS era, but one of the old-school leather bars that remains is the **SF Eagle** on Folsom, South of Market. Dancing is still the attraction, but the Eagle also hosts "Drag King" and "Mr. Leather" contests, wild affairs that usually benefit AIDS organizations.

For the girls... Many of the city's lesbian bars have closed or evolved into one-night clubs that move from location to location, but two have survived. The Bernal Heights bar **Wild Side West** is a quiet, out-of-the-way respite from the bustling city, where women can shoot a game of pool in homey surroundings. The backyard features toilets with flowers growing from the bowls. A more frenzied environment is **The Cafe** (formerly the Cafe San Marcos), a dark glass-and-chrome complex where the dance floor is usually as packed as the bar. Take a break from the action and enjoy a view from the balcony, which looks out over the Market and Castro intersection.

Drag and beyond... Since this is San Francisco, don't expect there to be just categories for gays, straights, and lesbians. Latina drag queens gravitate to **Esta Noche** in the Mission, sandwiched between burrito shops and liquor stores, where live shows run every weekend. The **Motherlode** in the Tenderloin caters to the transgender community, and weekends the picture windows on the corner are packed with all manner of put-together gals for lip-synch shows and other mayhem.

Where to take a date... For a first date with a twist of irony, the **Embers** is a great starting place, thanks to its unsettling parade of clown decorations. To establish your with-it, goateed credentials, head straight to the **Red Room**. If any of the other bars in this list don't sound cozy enough, we recommend the **Lone Palm**, on 22nd Street in the Mission, where all the tablecloths have candles, the tropical motif is nicely understated, and jazz plays softly enough that you can have a conversation. The crowd is quiet yet animated, strangely adult, and although it's not essential, some are even dressed up for the occasion. Also in the Mission, right next door to the Roxie Cinema revival house, is **Dalva**, a long, dark, narrow space with high ceilings and wrought-iron accents. Near many restaurants and clubs, it's quiet enough to have candles on the tables but loud enough for a deejay to spin everything from low-impact hip hop to Lou Reed. A picture window looks out onto busy 16th Street.

Where to take a meeting... If it's on the company dime, soak that expense account with a visit to the **Occidental Grill**, and see for yourself what the big martini deal is all about. If you personally have to get the bill, try **Tosca** early enough in the evening to avoid the thump from the next-door disco. Keep in mind, Tosca doesn't open until 5pm. (See The Cafe Scene.)

Best happy-hour food... If you like Mexican food, the barnlike **Cadillac Bar** hosts a complimentary buffet every weekday afternoon from 4:30 to 6:30, with nachos, burritos, chimichangas, and more. **MacArthur Park** caters to the Financial District and neighboring ad agencies and features on-the-house goodies like pasta salads and buffalo wings Monday through Friday, 5 to 7. And if you find yourself peckish in the Mission, **El Rio** forks out free oysters on the half shell every Friday afternoon.

SAN FRANCISCO ⟨ THE BAR SCENE

The Index

Armadillo's. Typical Lower Haight beer den with an Old West spin—pool, pints, and pit bulls.... *Tel 415/553–8953. 200 Fillmore St.; 6, 7, 22, 66, 71, 73 MUNI bus.*

Balboa Cafe. Pedigreed children of industry titans flash the plastic to get pink-faced and dance on the tables, which are tastefully covered by white tablecloths.... *Tel 415/921–3944. 3199 Fillmore St.; 22, 43 MUNI bus.*

Ben Butler Bar. The furthest west you can get, complete with seagulls and tour buses. Get a couple under your belt and visit the antique mechanized-toy museum.... *Tel 415/386–3330. 1090 Point Lobos Ave., in the Cliff House; 38, 38L, 38AX MUNI bus.*

Bruno's. A former Italian spaghetti joint turned vanguard of the so-called "cocktail nation," this place ranks among the best for highballs and live jazz.... *Tel 415/550–7455. 2389 Mission St.; 24th St. BART/MUNI Metro stop; 14, 14L, 26 MUNI bus.*

Buena Vista Cafe. Birthplace of Irish coffee, and an oasis for tourists tired from shopping on the Wharf. Nevertheless, a great view of the bay.... *Tel 415/474–5044. 2765 Hyde St.; 19 and 30 MUNI bus, Hyde St. cable car.*

Cadillac Bar. A cavernous Mexican restaurant tucked in an alley one block from the Moscone Convention Center, filled with rowdy visiting suits and downtowners. Does a big birthday-party business.... *Tel 415/543–8226. 325 Minna St.; 9X, 14, 14L, 30, 45 MUNI bus.*

The Cafe. By women, for women, but if you're a guy they won't kick you out. A commanding second-story balcony view of

Market, especially on Halloween night in the Castro.... *Tel 415/861–3846. 2367 Market St.; Castro St. MUNI Metro stop; 8, 24 MUNI bus.*

Cafe Mars. Industrial-design stop for martinis after work, in the heart of South of Market.... *Tel 415/621–6277. 798 Brannan St.; 19, 27 MUNI bus.*

City Tavern. One elbow of the Bermuda Triangle in the Marina. Lots of glass gives the sensation of "How much is that yuppie in the window?".... *Tel 415/567–0918. 3200 Fillmore St.; 22, 43 MUNI bus.*

Covered Wagon. The original guitar-rock South of Market dive, painted black to hide things you shouldn't see. A favorite of bike messengers, although you also bump into the occasional attorney.... *Tel 415/974–1585. 917 Folsom St.; 12, 27 MUNI bus.*

Cuddles. The Transbay Terminal ain't Grand Central Station, but this place is the only old-time transit bar we have left. Full of commuters and transients. Worth a visit just to check out the weird businesses throughout the lobby.... *Tel 415/543–7459. 425 Mission St.; 12, 14, 14L, 15 MUNI bus.*

Dalva. A Mission hotspot for hispters who can't afford martinis at the Red Room. It can turn into a scene on weekends.... *Tel 415/252–7740. 3121 16th St.; 16th St. BART/MUNI Metro stop; 22, 26 MUNI bus.*

Doctor Bombay's. Dank Mission chalet where ponytailed guys pound the shots of Jager, and girls pretend they're not. Note: this bar is never full.... *Tel 415/431–5255. 3192 16th St.; 16th St. BART/MUNI Metro stop; 22, 26 MUNI bus.*

Double Play. Hamburgers by day, neighborhood sports nuts by night. Sooner or later, you'll bump into the mayor.... *Tel 415/621–9859. 2401 16th St.; 22, 27, 33 MUNI bus.*

Edinburgh Castle. Live theater and music upstairs, single-malt scotches and lime-and-lagers on the ground floor. A favorite of everyone from sports teams to writers and neighborhood regulars. And if you're so inclined, a block's walk to gay hustlers or straight porn theaters.... *Tel 415/885–4074. 950 Geary Blvd.; 38, 38L MUNI bus.*

Embers. Hundreds of clown paintings, uncomfortable seating, and ceilings stained with nicotine are exactly why this place is popular. Retired tipplers in the afternoons give way to urban cool at night. Extra points for chain-smokers.... *Tel 415/731–8270. 627 Irving St.; on MUNI N line.*

Enrico's. Outdoor seating and live jazz make this North Beach landmark a natural habitat for forty- and fifty-somethings, district attorneys, and Eurotrash tourists.... *Tel 415/982– 6223. 504 Broadway St.; 15, 30, 41 MUNI bus.*

Esta Noche. Where the señores would really like to be señoritas, by any means necessary. Latin drag at its down-and-dirty finest.... *Tel 415/861–5757. 3079 16th St.; 16th St. BART/MUNI Metro stop; 22, 26 MUNI bus.*

Expansion. One of the best value dives, where the faces you see in the afternoon seem to be the same faces you see after dark. Odd contrast of liver-spotted patrons and the Allman Brothers on the jukebox. You know a bar has been around a long time when they just plain refuse to serve beer on tap.... *Tel 415/863–4041. 2124 Market St.; Church St. MUNI Metro stop; 8, 24 MUNI bus.*

500 Club. Opens at 6am. Booth seating. Bowling shirts. Pinball. What more do you need?.... *Tel 415/861–2500. 500 Guerrero St.; 22, 33 MUNI bus.*

Ginger's Trois. Downscale Financial District crowd, leaning toward gay. Garish Christmas lights, show tunes on the jukebox, Duraflame logs in the fireplace.... *Tel 415/989– 0282. 246 Kearny St.; 9X, 15 MUNI bus.*

Gino & Carlo. Big-screen sports above the bar, and in the back, small-time billiards. A classic slice of Italian North Beach, full of characters.... *Tel 415/421–0896. 548 Green St.; 15, 30, 41 MUNI bus.*

Gold Dust. Live Dixieland jazz, in Union Square where it belongs. Predominantly tourist, but you can't help but have fun where there's a banjo.... *Tel 415/397–1695. 247 Powell St.; 38, 38L MUNI bus; Powell St. cable car.*

Gordon Biersch Brewery. Yupscale microbrew scene that, according to one bartender, is quiet on the weekends, but during the week you see the singles and mistresses. Wear black and look over your shoulder a lot.... *Tel 415/243–8246. 2 Harrison St.; 82X, 80X MUNI bus.*

Harry Denton's Starlight Room. Uptown and upstairs, the top of the refurbished Sir Francis Drake gives you a commanding view of the city, in full clutch-purse-and-cummerbund glory. Check your hair in the mirror, and run this tab on the plastic.... *Tel 415/395–8595. 450 Powell St., in the Sir Francis Drake Hotel; 2, 3, 4, 76 MUNI bus; Powell St. cable car.*

Harvey's. Formerly the Elephant Walk, now the Hard Rock Cafe of gay memorabilia, named for assassinated city supervisor Harvey Milk. Of interest to tourists but an embarrassment to the local gay population.... *Tel 415/431–4278. 500 Castro St.; Castro St. MUNI Metro stop; 8, 24, 33 MUNI bus.*

Icon Byte Bar & Grill. Contrived shrine to the cyber revolution, with circuit-board decor and Internet connection. If you hang out here, you're not part of the solution, you're part of the problem.... *Tel 415/861–2983. 299 9th St.; 12, 19 MUNI bus.*

Ireland's 32. Great start for an Irish bar tour of the Richmond district. Many beers on tap, live music on weekends, and often, real Irish people.... *Tel 415/386–6173. 3920 Geary Blvd.; 38, 38L, 44 MUNI bus.*

Jack's. Old black blues bar now crowded with white-kid spillover from the Fillmore music hall and the local Kabuki movie theater complex. Excellent live acts, and the starting point for the award-winning chain of Jack's microbrew bars, including branches in the Mission and on the Wharf.... *Tel 415/567–3227. 1601 Fillmore St.; 22, 38, 38L MUNI bus.*

Johnny Love's. Singles scene with wacky drink recipes and limos out front. Makes you feel like you're back at Stanford, even if you didn't go there.... *Tel 415/931–8021. 1500 Broadway St.; 19, 30X MUNI bus.*

Kezar Club. Ceilings crowded with sports jerseys. The big sports stop for neighborhood armchair quarterbacks.... *Tel 415/386–9292. 770 Stanyan St.; 7, 33 MUNI bus.*

Lefty O'Doul's. One of the last piano bars that also serves buffet-style meat platters. Elbow up to the bar between vacationing grandparents and grizzled regulars examining their racing forms.... *Tel 415/982–8900. 333 Geary Blvd.; 38, 38L MUNI bus; Powell St. cable car.*

Li Po. Quintessential Chinatown bar, where you can easily get waylaid by one of their house concoctions. Home to North Beach hipsters as well as tourists who stumble in by accident.... *Tel 415/982–0072. 916 Grant Ave.; 15, 30, 41 MUNI bus.*

Lloyd's. A shot and a beer are $1.50. That's about it.... *Tel 415/431–9467. 1099 Mission St.; 14, 14, 26 MUNI bus.*

Lone Palm. Quiet, calm cocktails in the Mission. Tasteful tablecloths and candles suggest you straighten your posture, or at least light the lady's cigarette. A retreat for couples and other survivors who now drink like adults.... *Tel 415/648–0109. 3394 22nd St.; 26 MUNI bus.*

Lucky 13. Long, dim bar with many beer taps, filled with admin. assists. and temps who show their hatred for work by wearing Doc Martens every day.... *Tel 415/487–1313. 2140 Market St.; Church St. MUNI Metro stop; 8, 24 MUNI bus.*

MacArthur Park. Big picture windows that overlook Jackson Square Park. Lunch for the cell-phone execs from Levi-Strauss, who then return for cocktails after work.... *Tel 415/398–5700. 607 Front St.; 41 MUNI bus.*

Mad Dog in the Fog. Despite the British ale and fierce dart games, you're still in the goatee gulch known as the Lower Haight. But that's not so bad—you could be in Britain. Pull up a chair, order a plate of bangers, and hoot along with the crowd at the televised soccer matches.... *Tel 415/626–7279. 530 Haight St.; 6, 7, 22, 66, 71, 73 MUNI bus.*

M & M. Newspaper bar, a block from both daily papers. Opens early to prime the pump for delivery drivers and late-shift pressmen. And of course, reporters.... *Tel 415/362–6386. 198 5th St.; 12, 27 MUNI bus.*

The Mint. Four words: brightly lit gay karaoke. And also, it's louder than hell.... *Tel 415/626–4726. 1942 Market St.; 8 MUNI bus.*

Motherlode. Always a passel of gals sitting at the bar primping themselves, but remember: Hairy arms and size-12 feet usually indicate someone in a state of transition.... *Tel 415/928–6006. 1002 Post St.; 2, 3, 4, 19 MUNI bus.*

N Touch. Quiet, mellow neighborhood crowd, primarily Asian gay men and those who like them.... *Tel 415/441–8413. 1548 Polk St.; 1, 19 MUNI bus.*

Occidental Grill. Financial District spot specializing in martinis, cigars, and booths with curtains. If anybody still has the time these days for the highball lunch before heading back to the office, they come here.... *Tel 415/834–0484. 453 Pine St.; 12, 15 MUNI bus; California St. cable car.*

Persian Aub Zam Zam. Martinis for masochists only. This Upper Haight institution is open, closed, full, or empty whenever Bruno the bartender feels like it.... *Tel 415/861–2545. 1633 Haight St.; 6, 7, 33, 43, 66, 71, 73 MUNI bus.*

Pied Piper. Elegant drinking in one of the city's oldest hotels. And just look at that original Maxfield Parrish painting behind the bar.... *Tel 415/392–8600. Palace Hotel, Market and New Montgomery Sts.; Montgomery St. BART/MUNI Metro stop; almost every MUNI bus.*

Pier 23. A breezy, sunny bar/restaurant that, since it's San Francisco, can turn windy and freezing without warning. Locals sit at the bar facing the water, discussing boats they'd like to own someday.... *Tel 415/362–5125. Pier 23; 82X MUNI bus.*

Pierce Street Annex. Once a famous hippie joint called the Matrix, now a down-to-earth neighborhood pickup joint, filled with office workers who follow the best-selling music.... *Tel 415/567–1400. 3138 Fillmore St.; 22, 43 MUNI bus.*

Red Room. A *Details* magazine fashion shoot, with decor all completely the color red. A jazzy retro crowd devoted to black clothing, goatees, and backpacks the size of condoms.... *Tel 415/346–7666. 827 Sutter St.; 2, 3, 4, 27 MUNI bus.*

Redwood Room. Hushed except for the jazz pianist, with beautiful walls of—you guessed it, redwood. Business associ-

SAN FRANCISCO ⟋ THE BAR SCENE

ates, wealthy couples passing through town, and people like you, who probably can't afford it.... *Tel 415/775–4700. Geary and Taylor Sts., in the Clift Hotel; 27, 38, 38L MUNI bus.*

El Rio. Deep in the Mission, where women shoot pool, and the weekends are crowded with gay and straight dancing out on the patio. Friendly house cats lounge on the deck in the afternoons.... *Tel 415/282–3325. 3158 Mission St.; 14, 14L, 26, 49 MUNI bus.*

Rite Spot. Potrero bar and restaurant amid the warehouses. After-hours spot for the local theater community, hashing out the details of their latest productions.... *Tel 415/552–6066. 2099 Folsom St.; 12, 33 MUNI bus.*

La Rondalla. A must-see Mexican bar/restaurant, simply for its sense of utter chaos. You can smell the margaritas for blocks away. A local family plays live mariachi.... *Tel 415/647–7474. 901 Valencia St.; 26 MUNI bus.*

Saloon. North Beach blues bar that some say is the oldest bar in the city, even surviving the 1906 quake. The building looks like it may not survive the next big one, but this beer-soaked bunch doesn't care—the band's playing "Shotgun" by Joe Louis Walker.... *Tel 415/989–7666. 1232 Grant Ave.; 15, 41 MUNI bus.*

San Francisco Brewing Company. This historic North Beach brewpub draws after-hours office drones as well as the curious tourist, with live music and comedy every night. Brick walls, wooden ceiling fans, and "brew cubes" available to go.... *Tel 415/434–3344. 155 Columbus Ave.; 15, 41 MUNI bus.*

7-11 Club. Financial District dive attracting those for whom atmosphere is a low priority. Potentially depressing, unless you know what you're doing.... *Tel 415/777–4455. 711 Market St.; Powell St. BART/MUNI Metro stop; 9, 30, 71 MUNI bus.*

SF Eagle. The first word in San Francisco leather bars, and the last stop at the annual S&M-themed Folsom Street Fair. God knows what kind of activities have taken place here over the years.... *Tel 415/626–0880. 398 12th St.; 9, 12, 27 MUNI bus.*

Spec's 12 Adler Museum Cafe. Bare wood bar and tables let you know this is as good as it gets for this North Beach beatnik dive. Draft beers include only one: Budweiser.... *Tel 415/421–4112. 12 Adler St.; 15, 41 MUNI bus.*

Tarr & Feathers. Wooden walls, live music, hundreds of white T-shirts and blue Gap jeans, and Jager, Jager, Jager.... *Tel 415/563–2612. 2140 Union St.; 22, 41, 45 MUNI bus.*

Tommy's Mexican Restaurant. People come here because they already know what they're looking for—more types of tequila than anyone ever knew existed. Don't spread it around.... *Tel 415/387–4747. 5929 Geary Blvd.; 38, 38L MUNI bus.*

Toronado. Lower Haight working stiffs head here after cashing that paycheck, but the weekends attract microbrew novices, looking for their first glass of Fullers E.S.B.... *Tel 415/863–2276. 547 Haight St.; 6, 7, 22, 66, 71, 73 MUNI bus.*

Trad'r Sam. Traditional Tiki atmosphere out in the avenues, a mishmash of neighborhood regulars, thrill-seeking retro addicts, and people who actually like those bizarre bowls of rum disguised as drinks.... *Tel 415/221–0773. 6150 Geary Blvd.; 38, 38L MUNI bus.*

21 Club. Corner dive at the intersection of cheap drinks and overwhelming despair. Don't plan to stay here all night.... *Tel 415/771–9655.... 98 Turk St.; 31 MUNI bus.*

Twenty Tank Brewery. South of Market cacophony that occurs when you combine nearby music clubs, six types of fresh microbrews, two-story ceilings and frisky nine-to-fivers headed across the street to the Jonathan Richman show.... *Tel 415/255–9455. 316 11th St.; 9, 12 MUNI bus.*

Twin Peaks. Picture-window ambience as comfortable and boring as you can imagine; appeals to middle-aged and elderly gay men.... *Tel 415/864–9470. 401 Castro St.; Castro St. MUNI Metro stop; 8, 24 MUNI bus.*

Vesuvio. Beatnik-era decor now enjoyed by tourists who weren't even born before Jack Kerouac died. Hey, as long as he's still being read.... *Tel 415/362–3370. 255 Columbus Ave.; 15, 41 MUNI bus.*

Washington Square Bar & Grill. Legendary hangout of City Hall power brokers who wash down the veal scallopini with a few scotches and decide the future of the town's housing projects.... *Tel 415/982–8123. 1707 Powell St.; 15, 30, 41, 45 MUNI bus.*

Wild Side West. Primarily Bernal Heights lesbians, and anybody else who challenges the pool table. Walls of naked-women artwork.... *Tel 415/647–3099. 424 Cortland Ave.; 24 MUNI bus.*

Zeitgeist. Magnet for Euro bikers and bike messengers. Everything is painted black to hide the glitches.... *Tel 415/255–7505. 199 Valencia St.; 26 MUNI bus.*

Zeke's. Twenty years ago this was a hangout for Hunter S. Thompson and *Rolling Stone*rs. Now it's stomping grounds for the new generation of newspapers and magazines. And above everything else, it's still mostly a sports bar.... *Tel 415/392–5311. 600 3rd St.; 15, 30, 76 MUNI stop.*

The Haight & The Castro Bars

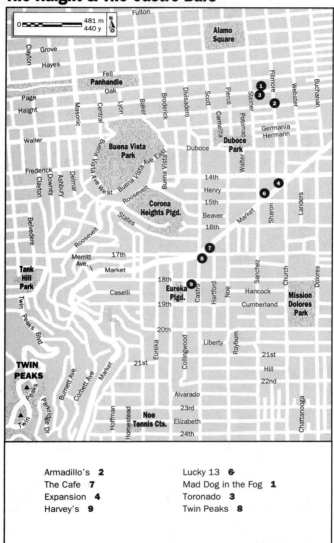

Armadillo's **2**	Lucky 13 **6**
The Cafe **7**	Mad Dog in the Fog **1**
Expansion **4**	Toronado **3**
Harvey's **9**	Twin Peaks **8**

San Francisco Bars

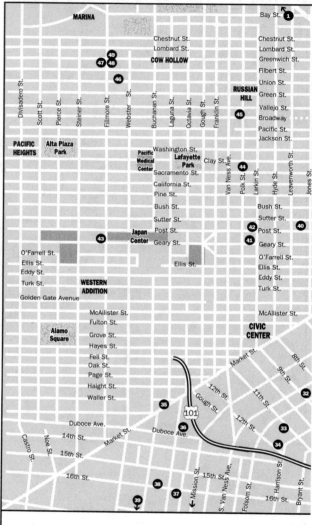

Balboa Cafe **47**	Enrico's **6**	Icon Byte Bar & Grill **32**
Buena Vista Cafe **1**	Esta Noche **37**	Jack's **43**
Cadillac Bar **24**	500 Club **39**	Johnny Love's **45**
Cafe Mars **29**	Ginger's Trois **15**	Lefty O'Doul's **18**
City Tavern **49**	Gino & Carlo **4**	Li Po **12**
Covered Wagon **27**	Gold Dust **19**	Lloyd's **31**
Cuddles **22**	Gordon Biersch Brewery **23**	MacArthur Park **11**
Doctor Bombay's **38**	Harry Denton's	M & M **26**
Edinburgh Castle **41**	Starlight Room **16**	

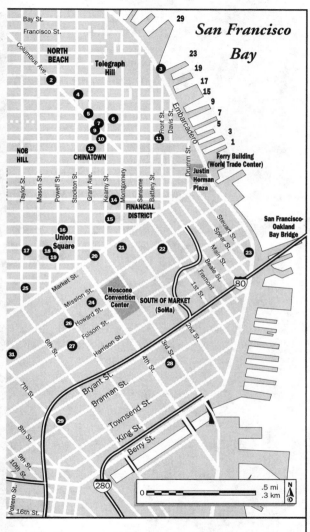

The Mint **35**
Motherlode **42**
N Touch **44**
Occidental Grill **14**
Pied Piper **21**
Pier 23 **3**
Pierce Street Annex **48**
Red Room **40**
Redwood Room **17**

Saloon **5**
San Francisco Brewing
   Company **10**
7-11 Club **20**
SF Eagle **34**
Specs 12 Adler
   Museum Cafe **7**
Tarr & Feathers **46**

21 Club **25**
Twenty Tank
   Brewery **33**
Vesuvio **9**
Washington Square
   Bar & Grill **2**
Zeitgeist **36**
Zeke's **28**

the cafe

scene 2

Like the old song says,
happiness is just a thing
called Joe…and sometimes
it seems like no one in this
town is really happy unless
they're walking around
with a take-out

cup. Or two. San Francisco is where the national coffee-culture craze was brewed up, and though such chains as Starbucks and Peets are colonizing every unspoken-for corner even here, the real deep-brewed flavor of cafe society draws from the life of the neighborhoods—just like everything else in San Francisco.

It's easier and cheaper, of course, to brew a pot at home, and with today's espresso makers you can conjure up perfect, flavored lattes and other gimmicky coffee drinks all by your lonesome.

But coffee is a social thing, and though San Francisco has an embarrassingly rich array of bars and restaurants, the neighborhood cafes—where everyone from the quarter-bumming slacker to the multimedia multimillionaire is admitted for the price of one coffee—are the true heart of the city. Not counting the chains (which will get no further attention here) there are more than 200 such places on the map.

In this town, the cafe has taken the place of the corner bar as the place where "everybody knows your name." In fact, given society's current low opinion of drinking and drugs, cafes have become the preferred hangouts for the cool-and-sober set. San Franciscans and visitors start the day in these de facto living rooms, and more often than not end it there, too.

Coffee culture in the city splits along the fault line between the more traditional sit-down cafes and coffeehouses and the trendy, theme-conscious coffee and espresso bars, which often add extra enticements like live music, poetry and performance, board games, and online computer networks.

Whichever sort of cafe you opt for, you'll find the locals gossiping, reading, scribbling journal entries...and sipping into the night.

The Lowdown

The old guard... If you like to take your coffee with history, sample the venerable Beat bistros of North Beach, exemplified by the 40-year-old **Caffe Trieste**, which has hosted the likes of Kerouac, Ginsberg, and Burroughs, along with many literary aspirants and groupies who make the pilgrimage for the thick atmosphere and thicker coffee. We like it, but the place has its detractors. The itinerant *Monk* magazine described it as "full of aging wannabe writers with hair ears who sit all day cruising chicks while contemplating their next paragraph as they absorb the cultural significance of being in this historical cafe where great minds once met." Another North Beach legend is the well-worn **Mario's Bohemian Cigar Store Cafe**, a corner of Italy bordering Washington Square Park, where you're quite likely to spot director Francis Ford Coppola pounding away at his PowerBook. When you've soaked up enough of the celebrity photos and authentically Italian ambience (and maybe a glass of the homemade *campari*), get a cup to go and sit on the church steps across the street for more neighborhood observations. At **Tosca**, media types from the business district a few blocks away mingle over *mochaccinos* in a heady atmosphere of opera (from the all-opera jukebox!) and old-fashioned Italian decor. Sure, $3 is a lot to pay for a cup of coffee, but remember, you're paying for that priceless North Beach atmosphere.

Haightin' it... If you'd rather score a bean buzz or contact-high with an authentic hippie vibe, head for the Haight, where the scent of espresso still wrestles with patchouli and other, um, herbal essences. **Sacred Grounds Cafe**, a former flophouse on the outskirts of Golden Gate Park, has kept the radical-chic spirit alive since 1972, with good, earthy food, slabs of redwood trees as furniture, and a mix of live music and poetry readings. Cross Divisadero into the Lower Haight, and you can dig the cozily countercultural **Love 'N' Haight** and **Horse Shoe Coffee House**, that still carry the torch for the "Summer of Love." The inexpensive Love 'N' Haight, encrusted with psychedelic art (including hundreds of hidden representations of the cafe's name), feels like a late-night hallucination, no matter what time it really is. Brothers Joel and Reham Haddad serve up good Middle Eastern food and salads there, plus the usual spread of pastries and coffees. The Horse Shoe is an anarchic all-day freak fest—bike-messenger nirvana. At night, there's usually some edgy live alternative music, and the funky, smoky, beyond–*Blade Runner* industrial clutter spills right out onto Haight Street.

Mission possible... The heavily Hispanic Mission district is also home to a huge slacker population (to "pass," drop by one of the area's multitude of thrift shops, score some Far Side glasses, a ratty cardigan or gas station jacket, and mess up your hair) and has a preponderance of homey, inexpensive, living room–style cafes. **Cafe Macondo** may be the purest expression of the type: smoky air diffusing the amber lamplight, South American art (from Catholic saints to shrunken heads) adorning the walls, and intense intelligentsia discussing relationships or the revolution amid mismatched thrift-shop furniture. Revolutionaries without a cause also flock to the airy, open **Café La Bohème**, one of the oldest cafes in the Mission. This is ground zero for the neighborhood's artistic underground: vivid, political art is often showcased on the walls, and the overflowing bulletin boards give a better picture of real life in the city than any of the local papers. Strangers often share the big wooden tables, whether for reading, journal-keeping, a chess game, or deep conversation. Every neighborhood deserves a mom-and-pop corner cafe like **Radio Valencia**, but unfortunately it's one of a kind. Owner and roots musicologist Don Alan plays songs from across the globe and musical spectrum in his one-room imaginary radio station (a card on each table notes tonight's playlist) and hosts a roster of acoustic bands till midnight. In 1995, a fire truck crashed in and took all of the cafe's prime window seats, along with the window itself, without a reservation (not that you need one here). Now rebuilt and repainted bright blue with gold trim, Radio Valencia's floor has been replaced with fire-engine-red linoleum to add just a touch of irony. The strongest brew in town, Max's Blend, is served nearby at **Muddy Waters**, where the walls are plastered with flyers for punk gigs, esoteric body work, and self-exploration schemes. Famous for its lethal brews, the coffeehouse also has every free paper known to San Francisco.

Piercing glances... That trendroid pouring your coffee at the **New Dawn Cafe** may sport more metal hardware than the espresso machine, but don't be scared: the natives are friendly and the big food is good and filling. The place looks like an explosion at Pee Wee's Playhouse: junk stacked on crap piled on tchotchkes atop knickknacks. (Hey—isn't that Jesus holding a pair of pom-poms behind the refills counter? And there's Santa under a hair dryer.) Somehow it's a good place to recover from The Morning After. Another outpost of the Modern Primitives and New Bohemians is **Red Dora's Bearded Lady Cafe and Gallery**, whose founder, Harriet, actually sports a little goatee. This cafe, art gallery, and performance space is owned, operated, and patronized by womyn-who-love-womyn, but it's a gender-neutral zone—if you can hang on the outskirts of sexuality, you're welcome. There's a limited vegetarian menu, it's smoke- and alcohol-free, and, of course, wheelchair-accessible (get your politically correct coffee here). While slugging coffee or a microbrew at **Brain Wash**, you can share fabric softener with a kitschy-cool crowd of imaginatively garbed, self-styled cyberkids and multimedia nerd-do-wells. The gossip quotient at this South of Market cybercafe/bar/laundromat makes it a good place to get the dirt while your Tide gets the dirt out. The Castro's **Bagdad Cafe**, nicknamed "Bad Hag" or "Fag Dad" by locals, collects nocturnal refugees from all corners of the city, so you never know who or what's going to be noshing next to you. It's a clean, well-lighted place serving breakfast around the clock, and you can enjoy the superb eavesdropping and people-watching opportunities as long as you like—you won't get kicked out as long as you order something.

Lattetude... Most cafes are informal and unpretentious, as a rule. But in a few of San Francisco's coffee spots, you've got to have a Look. If you're up for some competitive fabu-

SAN FRANCISCO ⟨ THE CAFE SCENE

lousness, try the Castro's cruisy indoor/outdoor **Café Flore** (known to cattier regulars as "Café Hairdo" or "Café Whore"). Power seat: left-hand corner as you walk in the Market Street entrance. The timid should sit on the line of patio benches and tables facing Market Street, where one can watch the show without being caught in the cross fire of stares and smoldering glances. Between the Castro and South of Market is an area known to locals as "Upper Safeway," which is where you'll find, in a tall Art Deco building, a stylishly timeless place called **The Orbit Room Cafe**. The habitués favor a retro look, the jukebox plays Astrid Gilberto, a James Bond theme, "Suspicious Minds"—a bit like stepping into the Twilight Zone for an espresso. But on nice nights, everyone drags the tables and chairs out of this time capsule and onto the sidewalk.

Exotica... The young at heart (and those just suffering from Peter Pan Syndrome) stay up way past their bedtimes in a Richmond coffeehouse-and–ice cream parlor called **Toy Boat**. For good reason. Its colorful, toy-strewn, multigenerational playpen ambience is just the cherry on top of a sundae that also includes fun rock music, good coffee, and fabulous (Double Rainbow) ice cream. You can even buy the toys to take home. The Mission district's **Cafe Istanbul**, a Byzantine mosaic of shimmering satin, brass sconces, faded tapestries, and dark-as-night coffee, is yet another world apart. Belly dancers make reservations essential on Wednesday and Saturday nights. Feeling adventurous? Try the pinkish Rose Syrup Latte, redolent of roses and coffee.

Of course, some avant-garde scenesters have already concluded that coffee is passé; tea is in. For those beyond coffee, **Mad Magda's Russian Tea Room**, in the antiques-and-boutiques neighborhood called Hayes Valley, takes tea a few steps beyond. In the front room, fortune-tellers will read your tarot cards, your palm, and of course, your tea leaves. You can also take your tea and scones into an unruly secret garden in back, lit with torches and year-round Christmas lights. Owner David Newmoyten, an opera singer, sometimes obliges his customers with an impromptu aria. Somehow it's fitting.

The Index

Bagdad Cafe. This glass-fronted Castro corner cafe is probably the most popular all-night and all-day spot in the city. Clean, well-lit, serves breakfast 24 hours a day.... *Tel 415/621–4434. 2295 Market St. at 16th St.; F streetcar, 8 Market MUNI bus.*

Brain Wash. A cybercafe, bar, and laundromat South of Market that resonates with cutting-edge gossip and eerie, otherworldly techno and ambient music.... *Tel 415/861–3663. 1122 Folsom St. between 7th and 8th Sts.; 12, 19 MUNI bus.*

Café Flore. No, you're not being paranoid: somebody IS watching you. At its cruisiest and gossipiest by day, this stylish, roomy indoor-outdoor cafe in the Castro is still a good spot to see and be scene after sundown.... *Tel 415/621–8579. 2298 Market St. at Noe St.; F streetcar, 8 Market MUNI bus.*

Cafe Istanbul. At night this Byzantine hangout in the Mission district glows like Aladdin's Cave. There's belly dancing on Wednesday and Saturday nights, and the Turkish coffees are memorably dark and bitter.... *Tel 415/863–8854. 525 Valencia St. between 16th and 17th Sts.; 6, 22, 53 MUNI bus.*

Café La Bohème. An old standby brimming with local art and Mission neighborhood life. Open and airy.... *Tel 415/285–4122. 3318 24th St. between Mission and Valencia Sts.; 24th St. BART/MUNI Metro stop; 14, 48, 49 MUNI bus.*

Cafe Macondo. The essential Mission cafe: thrift-shop furniture, smoky air, South American art, jazz or Spanish music, and a mix of Latinos and neighborhood bohemians.... *Tel*

415/863–6517. 3159 16th St. at Valencia St. Close to the Roxie Theater, 22 MUNI bus.

Caffe Trieste. A North Beach institution shared by old-timers, tourists, and plenty of wannabe artists hoping the Beats' creative juices came from an espresso cup.... *Tel 415/ 392–6739. 601 Vallejo St. at Grant Ave.; 15, 41 MUNI bus.*

Horse Shoe Coffee House. The home of "Extreme Coffee." Expect tattoos, nose rings, and loud alternative music all day and night at this Lower Haight hangout.... *Tel 415/ 626–8852. 566 Haight St. near Steiner St.; 22, 6, 7, 66, 71 MUNI bus.*

Love 'N' Haight. A psychedelic Lower Haight hangout serving good, inexpensive Middle Eastern food and salads, besides the normal cafe fare.... *Tel 415/252–8190. 553 Haight St. near Fillmore St.; 6, 7, 66, 22 MUNI bus.*

Mad Magda's Russian Tea Room. Fortune-tellers read tea leaves, palms, and tarot cards in the front room of this wild Hayes Valley cafe. In back is a wonderful torch-lit garden.... *Tel 415/864–7654. 579 Hayes St. near Laguna St., 21 MUNI bus.*

Mario's Bohemian Cigar Store Cafe. Authentically Italian, authentically Beat, and yes, that probably is Francis Ford Coppola working at a table in this North Beach institution on Washington Square.... *Tel 415/362–0536. 566 Columbus Ave. at Union St.; 15, 41, 30, 45 MUNI bus.*

Muddy Waters. True to its name, this Mission standby has one of the darkest, thickest, and most teeth-grindingly caffeinated brews in town—a disclaimer on the counter warns off the weak-hearted. But it's still not strong enough to make cramming-student, dread-headed-rocker, and lesbian-mom regulars blink.... *Tel 415/863–8006. 521 Valencia St. at 16th St., 16th St. BART/MUNI Metro stop.*

New Dawn Cafe. Riotous decor for Mission staff and space alike: eyebrow rings, birdcages, a giant, glowing pear, and a scabrous sign on the jukebox which we won't repeat. (Oh, yeah, good food and coffee, too).... *No telephone. 3174 16th St. between Valencia and Guerrero Sts., 22 MUNI bus.*

The Orbit Room Cafe. An Upper Safeway cafe in an Art Deco building. Retro is the look of choice. It's also right next door to the Little Hollywood Launderette, so you can duck in for a coffee between cycles.... *Tel 415/252–9525. 1900 Market St. between Herman and Guerrero Sts.; F streetcar, 37 MUNI bus.*

Radio Valencia. There's no broadcast signal and the owner takes no requests, but this cool mom-and-pop joint in the Mission is known as a great place to hear live and recorded music from around the globe. Ask about their memorable run-in with a fire truck in 1995.... *Tel 415/836–1199. 1199 Valencia St. at 23rd St.; 24th St. BART/MUNI Metro stop; 26, 48 MUNI bus.*

Red Dora's Bearded Lady Cafe and Gallery. A charming lesbian-run Mission district cafe, art gallery, and performance space, with a limited veggie menu and no smoking or alcohol. Among the pierced-and-tattooed regulars, keep an eye out for owner/performance artist Harriet, who sports a really cute little goatee.... *Tel 415/626–2805. 485 14th St. near Guerrero St., 26 MUNI bus.*

Sacred Grounds Cafe. A sixties relic in a former flophouse across the Panhandle from Haight Street. Serves good earthy food and a mix of live music and poetry readings.... *Tel 415/387–3859. 2095 Hayes St. at Cole St., 21 MUNI bus.*

Tosca. San Francisco loves its opera, and opera has always been the theme at this romantic, atmospheric North Beach cafe, with the world's classiest jukebox—all opera, all the time (the patrons often sing along).... *Tel 415/391–1244. 242 Columbus Ave. at Jackson St.; 15, 39, 41 MUNI bus.*

Toy Boat. Lots of people come to San Francisco in search of their inner child. They should start at this Richmond coffeehouse, essentially an inner toy box and ice cream parlor. Toys, coffee, and ice cream are all for sale.... *Tel 415/751–7505. 401 Clement St. at 5th Ave; 2, 44 MUNI bus.*

the

3

arts

"Heaven is a city like San Francisco." That's one of the more ringing, poignant, and hopefully, truthful lines from *Angels in America*, Tony Kushner's epic Tony- and Pulitzer prize–winning meditation on AIDS and progress in America, which was developed and premiered in San Francisco at the Eureka Theatre.

While the city may not be an arts nexus like New York or Los Angeles, there's no lack of things to see and hear and experience. Although the city's opinion of itself in matters cultural may be higher than it ought to be (it calls itself The City, for one thing, and you can actually hear the capital letters), there *is* a great deal of civic pride, which leads to great and broad-based support for the arts, largely unique among American cities. San Francisco is almost European in that way. Art is considered a major part of the all-important Quality of Life here. There's a high hotel tax, for instance, but fully 14 percent of that money goes to support for the arts. And S.F. claims to sell more theater tickets (per capita) than any other major American city.

But it's also very provincial, and very turned into itself. In the local theater scene, there's very little that's nationally established apart from such bigger companies as Berkeley Rep and **American Conservatory Theatre**. Still, lots of people want to express themselves theatrically here, and the result is as wide a range of quality as you will find in any city seemingly packed with people who want to put on plays. And San Francisco is quite intently focused on being a tourist town, so when you do have a big, gorgeous theater space like the A.C.T.'s recently restored Geary Theater, they tend to drag out the old faithfuls and recognizable name plays so visitors looking for something to do will take a chance. On the gay theater side, the few thoughtful plays are overwhelmed by trashy, sensational, and nudity-driven shows.

For serious music, the **San Francisco Symphony** has an excellent international reputation—while it's not one of the world's top ten, it will get there some day soon, thanks to young genius conductor Michael Tilson Thomas, who has revitalized its reputation. The city is also a national center for avant-garde music—composers John Adams and Paul Drescher live here, and the new-music scene has its own, very West Coast flavor—as well as for chamber music (the hip Kronos Quartet is based here) and early music, perhaps best represented by Nicholas McGeegan and the Philharmonia Baroque, who have a cultlike following.

As far as dance goes, the **San Francisco Ballet** is one of the best regional companies—it's not American Ballet Theatre or the New York City Ballet, but it's right up there. Then there's also the nearby Oakland and San Jose ballets—three classical companies are not bad for one area. In terms of modern dance, the Margaret Jenkins Dance Company and the Joe Goode Performance Group are the two to watch out for. Dance is a hot ticket here—everything sells out. But whatever you say about local theater you can say about local dance twice. Every other loft space in the Mission or SOMA is a dance studio, and there's more touchy-feely, cult-of-personality junk going on here than anywhere else. Some of the dance and performance stuff at **Theater Artaud** alone is enough to make you vote for Jesse Helms and Pat Buchanan. (Well, maybe not that drastic.)

San Francisco is also the home of high tech, and that multimedia influence often finds its way into performances, from the avant-garde dance/theater works of the technologically dazzling George Coates Performance Works to the **San Francisco Opera**.

Speaking of which, this is a big opera town. Opera is the oldest cultural tradition in S.F., dating back to its proud Old West days as a frontier Gold Rush town, when the Grand Opera was the epitome of civilization, and that was the thing to do. Still is. It's a city of opera queens—straight or gay, makes no difference (check out the enormous opera sections at the local Tower Records and Virgin Megastore). The pride of San Francisco, the world-class opera always sells out (so does the symphony, and often the ballet), which is one of many reasons it feels like you are living on Mars here—can you imagine that happening in any other American city, outside of New York?

S.F.'s legendary taste and tolerance for gender playfulness and the generally offbeat (or just Beat) make it a fertile breeding ground for experimental performance. People traditionally come to San Francisco to be untraditional, to find themselves, be themselves, and then express themselves. Among the artists who have emerged from San Francisco are comics-turned–movie stars Whoopi Goldberg and Robin Williams; Williams is still an active resident, and still shows up unannounced at comedy clubs to keep his stand-up energy fresh.

Sources

The most authoritative and comprehensive mainstream source for movie, theater, dance, and music listings is the "Datebook" tabloid in the Sunday *Chronicle*, better known as "the pink section" for the pink paper it's printed on. The movie and theater reviews also feature the "Little Man," an obnoxious homunculus icon who indicates whether a movie or

SAN FRANCISCO & THE ARTS

play is worth a standing ovation or missing entirely. For opera, classical music, and dance reviews, the *Chronicle*'s **Octavio Roca** is your man; for theater, the *Examiner*'s **Steven Winn** is usually on the money; for pop music, the *Chron*'s **Joel Selvin** is always enjoyable, if a bit too much in love with the city's sixties past. For listings and criticism with more attitude and a more avant-garde range, the indispensable free alternative weeklies the *Bay Guardian* and *SF Weekly* are distributed areawide every Wednesday morning, and are available almost everywhere you look in street boxes and in piles at cafes, clubs, restaurants, and laundromats. Neighborhood cafes also often have piles of flyers, as well as posters in the windows hawking nearby events. Radio stations that offer diverse programming and information on local performances and concerts include **KQED 88.5FM** (NPR), **KPFA 94.1 FM** (Pacifica News), **KPOO 89.5 FM**, and the rock-oriented **KFOG 104.5 FM**.

Getting Tickets

As for getting seats, the **TIX** Bay Area kiosk on the Stockton side of Union Square is the S.F. equivalent of New York's TKTS half-price tickets booth, offering half-price, cash-only tickets for theater, dance, and opera on the day of the show (they also sell full-price advance tickets, credit cards accepted). The **BBS Tickets** brokerage has outlets around the city (tel 800/225-2277), but you can be certain of paying a substantial "convenience charge." Calling the box office directly is probably your best bet for tickets.

In cases like opera and ballet, which are always sold out to season ticketholders, visitors still have options. First check the **box office** early in the morning of a performance for tickets returned that day. A limited number of $8 standing-room tickets are available for every performance. Get to the box office early in the morning and buy a numbered ticket; then return two hours before the performance to stand on your numbered spot (there are actually numbers painted on the sidewalk). When they open the doors, make a dash for the dress circle standing-room area—the best place to hang out, because you can see everything and it's not too far away (you can't see the projected surtitles from the orchestra standing-room section). If you miss out on standing room, there are always **scalpers** hanging around the box office area, hawking same-day tickets. For some reason, scalpers here are not as greedy as they are in other cities, and it's not illegal.

The Lowdown

Only In San Francisco... A few shows seem determined to become San Francisco landmarks. One that already has is the musical revue **Beach Blanket Babylon**, a must-see on the order of Pier 39 and Coit Tower, and a perennial San Francisco treat that even natives don't mind seeing again and again. Having survived the death of its creator, Steve Silver, the raucous, long-running gag-a-second musical comedy revue lampoons figures of the day, and is known for its trademark enormous hats, including the one worn by Mermanesque star Val Diamond (when she's in the show, which isn't always) featuring the entire city skyline. Christopher Durang's farce about lovelorn singles and their nutty shrinks, *Beyond Therapy*, which has notched seven years at various venues around town, and is currently at the Cinnabar Cabaret (tel 415/693–0600; 450 Geary St. on lower level), has become, for better or worse, the unofficial *Fantasticks* of San Francisco.

There's no biz like show biz... San Francisco's beautifully restored mainstream houses offer relatively little straight theater, opting instead for touring musical productions that are light on the mind and heavy on the entertainment. The **Curran Theatre** in Union Square is under the management of coproducers Carole Shorenstein Hayes (in S.F.) and James M. Nederlander (on Broadway), who have been using the Curran as home base for their "Best of Broadway" series. The Curran has been held hostage for months on end by such spectacular Andrew Lloyd Webber musicals as the unbudgeable *Phantom of the Opera*, which satisfies the tastes of the sort of tourists who go to Planet Hollywood on purpose. The acoustically awful rear balconies of this 1,678-seat theater are to be avoided if at all possible. Another part of the Shorenstein/Nederlander empire, the **Golden Gate Theatre**, on the fringe of the dramatic-in-its-own-way Tenderloin district, is a 2,400-seat 1922 landmark designed by G. Albert Lansburgh that recently underwent a glitzy face-lift. The fare is Broadway musicals on a more intimate, less intimidating scale, such as *Blood Brothers* and *The Will Rogers Follies*, and, of course, attractions change more often here than they do at the Curran.

Broadway revivals such as *West Side Story* and entertainers such as Johnny Mathis have played the plushy, ornate **Orpheum Theater**, once an important stop on the national vaudeville circuit. The 2,503-seat venue is roomy, but the sight lines are unfortunate, and the Tenderloin neighborhood is touch and go, so take a cab. Light musicals are what the people seem to want at Union Square's 800-seat **Theatre on the Square**, where the production standards land on a scale somewhere between off-Broadway and solid regional.

The play's the thing... Most of San Francisco's straight theater (we use the term in its nonsexual sense) is relegated to small, fringe production houses short on money but long on artistic motivation. The major exception is A.C.T.—**American Conservatory Theater**—which recently spent millions of dollars repairing and renovating the lovely Geary Theater, one of the landmarks seriously wounded in the October 1989 Loma Prieta earthquake. Going to the Geary is like going to the theater in London—you actually look forward to a long play with lots of intermissions—maybe an O'Neill or a Noël Coward piece—just so you can hang out in the graceful and grown-up lobby lounges in the basement mezzanine and balcony levels. The long, sweeping staircases, accented by arcing, twisting metalwork, are perfect for dramatic entrances, and the impressive windows onto Geary Street make a great backdrop for posing with a cocktail. Criticized by Bay Area performers for casting out-of-town talent and for programming too many tried-and-true crowd-pleasers (the new artistic director, Carey Perloff, was recruited from the New York theater scene), A.C.T. still offers a thoughtful theatergoing experience, in a gorgeous and civilized environment.

While the Geary Theater was being restored, the nearby **Stage Door Theatre** often served as A.C.T.'s home away from home; now the intimate space is again presenting offbeat (if crowd pleasing) comedies and musicals like *Medea: The Musical* and Steve Martin's hit, *Picasso at the Lapin Agile*.

There are no small theaters... Just small audiences. (Just kidding.) San Francisco has more than a few theaters whose artistic reputations far exceed what their budgets, square footages, or seat counts would indicate. Tucked into the Fort Mason arts-and-offices complex is the 170-seat **Magic Theatre**, which made a national name for itself as the home of many of Sam Shepard's early works in the 1970s. Shepard's moved on, but the Magic is cultivating new, young talent and still pulls dazzling new plays out of its hat a few times each season. Black playwrights have a forum and a showcase in the downtown **Lorraine Hansberry Theatre**, which presents experimental plays by up-and-coming writers while also mounting works by award-winning playwrights August Wilson and Charles Fuller and adaptations of works by Toni Morrison and Alice Walker. Snuggled in among the downtown theaters is **EXIT Theatre**, which serves up bite-sized comedies and avant-garde entrees in a cabaret setting (so you can have a glass of wine or beer with your existential chuckles). Finally, few theaters do as thorough a job of serving their neighbors as the **Mission Cultural Center for Latino Arts**, a small, community-centric space for contemporary and classical plays in Spanish and English, not to mention poetry readings, performance pieces, and other creative work for all ages.

Experimental (and just plain mental)... For more experimental fare, turn first to the out-of-the-way but well-respected **Theater Artaud**, which not only offers off-the-wall dance but work by such nationally established cutting-edge theater directors as Anne Bogart in a handsomely renovated warehouse near Potrero Hill. Every summer, Artaud hosts an annual weekend-long performance marathon, with caffeinated (and otherwise wired) artists creating round the clock. **The Marsh**, less out of the way in the Mission district, is a breeding ground for comedy and alternative solo performance pieces: Several off-Broadway successes, such as Charlie Varron's *Rush Limbaugh in Night School* and Josh Kornbluth's *Mathematics of Change*, were workshopped on its stage.

Boys will be girls or boys will be naked during many of the witty, gay (and lesbian) plays at the nationally-acclaimed **Theatre Rhinoceros**. But then, male nudity is a staple of some S.F. theater. The dramatists' justification: It expresses a character's vulnerability. The truth: It usually doesn't hurt the box office. The dependably deranged **Climate Theater**, home of the famous Solo Mio Festival of solo performers, spills forth some of the Bay Area's most creative fringe productions. There, you'll sit on the edge of your folding chair during shows ranging from improvisational soap operas to goth-rock sex-worker comedies. Danielle Willis, a prostitute with a tragic, pale-makeup-and-smeared-mascara look, had a one-woman show that ran here for more than a year; genderbender artist Justin Bond is also a frequent guest artist. The **Marilyn Monroe Memorial Theater** frequently stages very homegrown plays that comment on current trends or famous figures, such as girl gangs and Camille Paglia. (Those were two separate shows, by the way.)

Where Jesse Helms goes for fun... If you want to see drag queens and kings in all their fierce, funny glory, **Dragstrip** is *the* place, famous for its all-night extravaganzas at South of Market's DNA Lounge, featuring every genderfuck artist in town, from Pussy Tourette to Elvis Herselvis, doing his/her/its thing. At **Josie's Cabaret and Juice Joint** in the Castro, you can drink healthy stuff (juices, smoothies, teas) or alcohol and maybe even sit in the world's smallest balcony while gay and lesbian comics and performance artists work it all out on the tiny stage. The all-volunteer punk-rocker-run collective **Epicenter Zone** is part record-and-zine store, part performance space, and headquarters for the city's surviving—even thriving—punk scene, so you can hear bands here or witness some of the more extreme styles of piercing and performance; check out the bulletin board for fliers and posters about upcoming shows and events. **Intersection for the Arts**, S.F.'s oldest alternative arts center and birthplace of the early works of Sam Shepard and Whoopi Goldberg (not collaborations, mind you), is a struggling, community-oriented performance grab-bag space in the Mission. Confrontational, politically oriented work is an Intersection specialty. Too earnest for you? There's always something odd, shocking, and usually funny—like the all-queer revision of *West Side Story*—going on nearby at the vast, loftlike multiuse gallery/performance space called **The LAB**. Also in the Mission, **LunaSea** is a lesbian-run performance space hosting women-only readings, "switch" cabaret shows, and amateur strip nights—most of which double as fundraisers. **New Langton Arts** is primarily an interesting art gallery in SOMA, but it will often stage readings or performances around a theme—say, mental illness—related to the art exhibit.

What's opera, doc?... Like every other opera company in the country (hell, like every other cultural institution, period), the **San Francisco Opera** is going through financial hardship, but it has deep local support, and is one of the great companies in this country, with a tradition of trying out great singers (Leontyne Price and Frederica Von Stade among others) before they become famous. Casts here are always interesting—you'll see these singers at the Met two years later. And it's a favorite house for lots of singers (who probably also like it because there's so much great food in the Bay Area!). During the week, it's more dressy, a fur-and-tuxedo sort of thing, but on the weekends, it attracts out-of-town visitors and an amazingly eclectic bunch of opera-loving characters. A lot of people go just for the sheer physical experience of going to the beautiful building, which is being restored and seismically retrofitted after the damage of the 1989 Loma Prieta quake. Before restoration began, an "earthquake crack" tour of the opera house, with its dozens of grand marble stairways and foyers and oh-so-civilized lounges and lobby bars, was one of the true cultural-connoisseur treats of the city.

The San Francisco Opera has a few rivals as well, including **Pocket Opera** (tel 415/989–1855), which presents seldom-seen chamber operas and lighter pieces (often at Temple Emanu-El), and the **Lamplighters Music Theatre** (tel 415/227–0331; Presentation Theatre, 2350 Turk St. at Masonic), a well-loved and well-regarded Gilbert and Sullivan company.

Top of the cultural food chain... Like New York, San Francisco has a taste for high culture, and the ballet, symphony, and opera are all enormously popular. (It's almost un-American!) Although the crowds at these events usually consist of overdressed older folks looking for classy entertainment, each of these organizations is eager to attract a new audience and work the young urban hipster set with cool programming and special events. One tony refugee from the opera-house restoration is the **San Francisco Ballet**, known for its eclectic programming— a typical season offers works by Jerome Robbins or Mark Morris and classics like *Swan Lake*. The hip, young conductor Michael Tilson Thomas (or MTT, as he is known around here) has revitalized the **San Francisco Symphony**. Unlike the opera and the ballet, the symphony can and does take risks and perform obscure works simply for their artistic merit, and the addition of at least one new program every week means a huge repertoire. Exceptional playing, complemented by the sleek, modern Davies Symphony Hall, makes an MTT evening memorable. You won't fall asleep.

Men in tights... Only Manhattan is ahead of the Bay Area as a center of dance activity, and neighborhoods like the Mission and South of Market bristle with loft studios, experimental troupes, and ethnic dance groups. Emerging and avant-garde dance has a home at the very small, very alternative **848 Community Space**, and you can usually count on seeing a lot of hunky artistic director Keith Hennessey in one of his frequent wild and woolly performances. Movement is also the mission at the Mission's popular **Footwork Dance Studio**, which hosts the work of cutting-edge choreographers. Stand-out troupes to watch for include **O.D.C./San Francisco** (tel 415/863–6606) (which stands for Oberlin Dance Collective) presenting works by the group's noteworthy choreographers; the out-there, experimental **Margaret Jenkins Dance Company** (tel 415/863–1173); and the **Joe Goode Performance Group** (tel 415/648–4848), which, by its own estimation, "stretches the boundaries of dance and theater." Critics and audiences seem to agree. Estimable ethnic ensembles include **Theatre Flamenco of San Francisco** (tel 415/826–1305), **Rosa Montoya Bailes Flamenco** (tel 415/824–1960), and **Khadra International Folk Ballet** (tel 415/626–7360).

Classical sounds... Though the San Francisco Symphony towers over the serious music scene (see "Top of the Cultural Food Chain," above), there is plenty more going on in this music-minded town, from visiting symphonies and chamber and choral music recitals to avant-garde performances and festivals both indoors and out. **San Francisco Performances** (tel 415/398–6449) is a major presenter of classical music and dance events, and usually books them into **Herbst Theatre** (a short walk up the block from Davies Symphony Hall and the opera house) or the larger **Masonic Auditorium**, with its splendid acoustics, gorgeous nature-inspired sculptures, and monumental stained-glass murals by Big Sur artist Emile Norman. In the Fort Mason Center complex, **Cowell Theatre** has become a popular site for small classical ensembles, as has the newly restored and reopened **Palace of the Legion of Honor** in Lincoln Park. Neighborhood-based venues that frequently host "good music" include the Mission's **Community Music Center**, which books chamber ensembles along with jazz groups and world musicians, and the cozy, unpredictable **Noe Valley Ministry**, which is as likely to book folkies or punkers as string quartets and Eastern European choral groups.

Keep an ear cocked for performances by these hometown stars: The internationally celebrated men's choral group **Chanticleer** (tel 415/896–5877), which performs a dozen or so concerts in the area each year, often in the spectacular Mission Dolores Basilica or Grace Cathedral; the innovative **Kronos Quartet** (tel 415/731–3533), which introduced Jimi Hendrix to chamber music fans and usually appear at Herbst when they play their hometown; the **San Francisco Bach Choir** (tel 415/922–1645) and **San Francisco Chamber Symphony** (tel 415/495–2919); the **Slavyanka Chorus** (tel 415/979–8690), a male ensemble that performs an Eastern European a cappella repertoire; the **Philharmonia Baroque Orchestra** (tel 415/391–5252), which dotes on 17th- and 19th-century composers, and the **Women's Philharmonic Orchestra** (tel 415/543–2297), which concentrates on historical and contemporary works by female composers.

Groovy movies... San Francisco is mad about the movies, and the movies are mad about S.F. right back—after all, this is the location of such greats as *Dark Passage* with Bogie and Bacall, *The Maltese Falcon*, *Bullitt*, and *Dirty Harry* (oh, those San Francisco chase scenes!), near-greats like *The Towering Inferno* and *Interview With the Vampire*, and unmentionables like *Sister Act II*. But in the age of home video, going to the movies can seem less than elegant these days: People talk, munch popcorn, crinkle candy wrappers, and just generally behave as if they were watching a tape at home. But there's still no replacement—movies not only look and sound better in the theater, but the social experience often enhances the art.

In the sixties, S.F. was one of the birthplaces of underground cinema and the cult (or midnight) movie phenomenon. Midnight showings aren't as common today, but a wide variety of repertory houses and alternative, avant-garde sites are still around. **The Castro** shows brand-new prints of American and international classics and camp faves; a special treat is the preshow appearance by the snazzy old organist guy, who plays a few tunes on the theater's grand pipe organ while everyone's bringing snacks back to their seats, always finishing with "San Francisco," and disappearing hydraulically into the floor before the ornate curtains part for show time. The crowd eats it up. Hong Kong action flicks, provocative independent films and documentaries, and film noir classics have an appreciative home at the Mission's funky **Roxie Cinema**, outfitted with couches (San Francisco audiences LOVE couches); the atmosphere is seedier and the crowd rowdier. The **Red Vic Movie House** in the Haight is small and cozy; **The Casting Couch Micro Cinema** is smaller and cozier still, with great snacks. **S.F. Cinematheque** and the less-organized **Total Mobile Home Micro Cinema** host local and national experimental work. Right next door to a voodoo boutique, the Mission's funky storefront screening room **Artists' Television Access** shows forbidden films, rough-cut works in progress, and taboo-theme evenings, like drag queen Vaginal Creme Davis ("that's *Dr.* Vaginal Creme Davis, thank you very much") hosting a night of experimental Warholesque works or a whole night of movies about vomiting.

Oh yeah—you might even want to go to a first-run feature while you're here. A good place to see a new flick is the AMC **Kabuki 8 Theatres**, a conveniently located Japantown multiplex featuring two large screens and six smaller ones, with digital stereo THX sound. For a real retro treat, check out the well-maintained, double-screen **Century Geneva Drive-In** in nearby Daly City and bring your main squeeze, a blanket, and your own snacks. If you want to know what's playing (and when and where), dial **777-FILM**, for free info about movies, theaters, ticket prices, and show times.

Laugh's on you... The comedy-club boom of the eighties seems to have had its last laugh, maybe because so many of the circuit performers can be seen for free and around the clock on cable. But a few dependable venues for yucks and chuckles remain, including **Cobb's Comedy Club**, in the lower courtyard of the Cannery near Fisherman's Wharf, which books touring national performers. The **Punchline** on Battery Street is home to the annual San Francisco Comedy Competition, and its Sunday night comedy showcase, featuring Bay Area jokesters to watch, is a bargain at $5.

Spectacles and experiences... If you are the kind of eternal adolescent who's into sci-fi movies, giant out-of-control robots, model rockets, chemistry sets, and blowing things up, you'll want to keep an ear to the ground for one of the semi-illegal performances by Mark Pauline's world-famous **Survival Research Laboratories**, whose secret pyrotechnic events draw crowds of hundreds. Using scrap metal, scavenged industrial materials, and animals (living and dead), Pauline makes giant robots that attack each other and do battle with flaming oil barrels and the like. Audiences take life and limb into their own hands at SRL events, as flame-throwing machines tend to roam perilously close to the crowds. Experiencing the underground wildness of SRL takes connections, persistence, and more than a bit of right-time, right-place luck. First you have to hear about one of the secretly planned events, which are often shut down by police, so invitations are usually by word of mouth and on the Internet a few hours before the show. Try the SRL website, which gives you a preview of founder Mark Pauline's monstrous machines at work (http://www.srl.org). Two other inimitable S.F. arts spectacles also have a techie edge, but they're a little more tame. At **Audium**, a domed room with floating floors and a suspended ceiling, listeners sit in the dark in concentric circles while free-form compositions are created live by a tape performer—a sort of Great and Powerful Oz man-behind-the-curtain—who "sculpts" and directs sounds through the room's 169 speakers. The **Laserium** light show, performed in the planetarium in the Academy of Sciences at Golden Gate Park, trips visitors out under the influence of more familiar aural fare, like Pink Floyd's "Dark Side of the Moon," Nirvana, or the Grateful Dead.

The Index

American Conservatory Theater. Having recently returned to the restored landmark Geary Theater, A.C.T. continues to mean serious theater. Relying heavily on tried-and-true popular plays, A.C.T. occasionally redeems itself by going out on a limb.... *Tel 415/749–2228. Geary Theater, 415 Geary St. between Mason and Taylor Sts.; Powell St. BART/MUNI Metro stop; F streetcar; Powell-Hyde and Powell-Mason cable car; 2, 3, 4, 76 MUNI bus.*

Artists' Television Access. Media arts center in a low-budget setting (folding chairs, a small pull-down screen) for low-budget experimental shorts. A weekly event called Other Cinema shows media pranks like Todd Hayne's brilliant, banned *Superstar: The Karen Carpenter Story*, with its cast of Barbie dolls. Typical subject matter any night of the week: radical politics, kinky sex, bloody surgeries.... *Tel 415/824–3890. 992 Valencia St. at 21st St.; 26 MUNI bus.*

Audium. Up for some aural sex? At Audium, listeners are enveloped by 169 speakers as a tape performer "sculpts" original and very free-form musical compositions.... *Tel 415/771–1616. 1616 Bush St. near Van Ness Ave.; California cable car; 2, 3, 4, 42 MUNI bus; Fri, Sat at 8:30.*

Beach Blanket Babylon. A San Francisco landmark on par with the Golden Gate Bridge, Coit Tower, and the Transamerica Pyramid—all of which show up atop one of this musical comedy revue's enormous trademark hats.... *Tel 415/421–4222. Club Fugazi, 678 Green St. between Columbus Ave. and Powell St.; 15, 30, 41, or 45 MUNI bus.*

The Casting Couch Micro Cinema. "The world's first micro theater" (just 46 seats) is a unique place to nuzzle your date, kick back in the comfy chairs and overstuffed couches, and be served hors d'oeuvres and drinks by a cute waiter. Gay-owned and gay-friendly, the Couch specializes in movies that would normally never get exposure (and movies that never got the exposure they deserved). Cost is usually $8.50 plus drinks and snacks.... *Tel 415/986–7001. 950 Battery St. between Green and Vallejo Sts., 42 MUNI bus.*

The Castro. San Francisco's most successful revival theater relies heavily on American favorites—Scorsese, Altman—to draw the crowds, but the pipe organist who entertains before showings is one of many personal touches that keeps 'em coming back for more. Plan your trip to S.F. around the annual October showing of *The Wizard of Oz*, a citywide event—you'll feel like you've never seen it before.... *Tel 415/621–6120. 429 Castro St. between Market and 18th Sts.; Castro BART/MUNI Metro stop; F streetcar; 24, 37 MUNI bus.*

Century Geneva Drive-In. A real drive-in picture show! Two screens, parked by the water, next to the Cow Palace. Take a six-pack of something, blankets for the back seat, and you're ready for a dream date.... *Tel 415/587–2884. 607 Carter St., Daly City.*

Climate Theater. Dark, cozy South of Market birthplace of some of the Bay Area's more creative fringe productions. Shows a range, from improv soap operas to goth-rock sex-worker comedies, from drag ensemble pieces to solo performance works. The stage is small, the seats elevated, the performers deranged and proud.... *Tel 415/978–2345. 252 9th St. between Folsom and Howard Sts.; Civic Center BART/MUNI Metro stop; F streetcar; 12, 19, 42 MUNI bus.*

Cobb's Comedy Club. Touring stand-up comics usually stop here. Triple bills are commonplace; a three-hour marathon showcase (featuring 14 yuksters) happens every Monday.... *Tel 415/928–4320. 2801 Leavenworth St. at Jefferson St., in the Cannery complex, S. bldg, courtyard entrance; 32, 42 MUNI bus.*

Community Music Center. Mission district rehearsal hall and performance space that plays host to chamber music ensembles.... *Tel 415/647–6015. 544 Capp St. at 20th St.; 16th St. BART/MUNI Metro Stop, 14 MUNI bus.*

SAN FRANCISCO ⟨ THE ARTS

Cowell Theatre. Elegant bayfront venue for small classical ensembles and occasional one-person theatrical performances.... *Tel 415/441–5706. Fort Mason Center, Pier 2, Laguna St. at Marina Blvd., 28 MUNI bus.*

Curran Theatre. Located in Union Square amid the city's most popular hotels, the Curran hosts the spectacular Andrew Lloyd Webber musicals tourists love.... *Tel 415/474–3800. 445 Geary St. between Mason and Taylor Sts.; Powell BART/MUNI Metro stop; F streetcar; Powell-Hyde and Powell-Mason cable car; 2, 3, 4, 38 MUNI bus.*

Dragstrip. Emcee/host(ess) Lu Read's monthly pansexual nightspot is an eye-popping, ear-filling parade of drag queens, drag kings, and strippers.... *Tel 415/331–9595, ext. 300. At DNA Lounge, 375 11th St. at Harrison St.; 12, 42 MUNI bus.*

848 Community Space. Touchy-feely improvisational experimental dance still has a home here. Some performers are gay, some are feminist, some are spiritual in a pagan way, some are all that and more.... *Tel 415/922–2385. 848 Divisadero St. at McAllister St.; 5, 24 MUNI bus.*

Epicenter Zone. A drop-in center for tuned-in dropouts and other artsy slackers. Includes a library, a bunch of bins crammed with obscure music, and space for radical arts events.... *Tel 415/431–2725. 475 Valencia St. at 16th St.; 16th St. BART/MUNI Metro stop; 22, 26 MUNI bus.*

EXI Theatre. Performance, poetry readings, neighborhood variety shows, in a tiny folding-chair space in the Tenderloin. Home of the annual San Francisco Fringe Festival.... *Tel 415/673–3847. 366 Eddy St. at Leavenworth St.; Powell BART/MUNI Metro stop; F streetcar; 19, 31, 37 MUNI bus.*

Footwork Dance Studio. Emerging and avant-garde dance presented in a Mission district loft.... *Tel 415/824–5044. 3221 22nd St. at Bartlett St.; 26 MUNI bus.*

Golden Gate Theatre. Whereas the Curran presents *The Phantom of the Opera*, this venue on the fringe of the Tenderloin presents *Blood Brothers*—Broadway musicals of a smaller, less intimidating scale.... *Tel 415/474–*

3800. 1 Taylor St. between 6th and Market Sts.; Civic Center BART/MUNI Metro stop; F streetcar; 5, 19, 31, 37 MUNI bus.

Herbst Theatre. Small-scale art deco performance hall that's home to the famous Kronos Quartet, the not-quite-as famous San Francisco Chamber Symphony, and a good lecture series as well.... Tel 415/621–5344. Veterans Building, 401 Van Ness Ave. at McAllister St.; Van Ness BART/MUNI Metro stop; F streetcar; 5, 42 MUNI bus.

Intersection for the Arts. Birthplace of the early works of Sam Shepard and Whoopi Goldberg, S.F.'s oldest alternative arts center is a community-oriented performance grab-bag space, with an art gallery and theater.... Tel 415/626–2787. 446 Valencia St. near 16th St.; 16th St. BART/MUNI Metro stop; 22, 26 MUNI bus.

Josie's Cabaret and Juice Joint. Queer-friendly cabaret space with a tiny stage that welcomes new plays, local and nationally known comedians like Marga Gomez and Jaffe Cohen, drag artistes like The Fabulous Lypsinka, and really entertaining open-mike nights.... Tel 415/861–7933. 3583 16th St. at Market St.; Castro BART/MUNI Metro stop; F streetcar; 24, 37 MUNI bus. No credit cards.

AMC Kabuki 8 Theaters. Modern, AMC cineplex in Japantown boasting comfy seats, stellar sound, and a popular series of midnight movies. Espresso, sushi, and ice cream are served—just don't eat them all together, or if you do, don't sit next to us.... Tel 415/931–9800. 1881 Post St. at Fillmore St.; 2, 3, 22, 38 MUNI bus.

The LAB. This home for postmodern art with a comic edge is an art gallery by day. Typical of the site's infrequent evening entertainment: Staged readings of plays by local novelist Kevil Killian, featuring S.F. scenesters as famous Hollywood stars.... Tel 415/863–2989. 2948 16th St. at Capp St.; 16th St. BART/MUNI Metro stop, 22 MUNI bus.

Laserium. A trippy live laser-light show set to, say, Pink Floyd, Nirvana, or the Grateful Dead.... Tel 415/750–7138. In Morrison Planetarium, in the California Academy of Sciences, Golden Gate Park; 24, 44 MUNI bus.

SAN FRANCISCO & THE ARTS

Lorraine Hansberry Theatre. Produces plays by leading black playwrights and collaborates with other S.F.-area companies on larger works.... *Tel 415/474–8800. 620 Sutter St. at Mason St.; Powell-Hyde and Powell-Mason cable car; 2, 3, 4, 76 MUNI bus.*

LunaSea. Part of a busy Mission district feminist/lesbian art scene. Most shows are fundraisers that cram a bunch of short works onto one big bill.... *Tel 415/863–2989. 2940 16th between Capp St. and South Van Ness Ave., room 216C; 16th St. BART/MUNI Metro stop; 22, 33, 53 MUNI bus.*

Magic Theatre. Sam Shepard is the best-known success story of this well-established font of new cutting-edge works.... *Tel 415/441–8822. Fort Mason Center, Bldg. D, Laguna St. at Marina Blvd.; 28 MUNI bus.*

Marilyn Monroe Memorial Theater. The folks who run this place, Peter Carlaftes and Kathi Georges, frequently write and produce their own plays, which comment on current trends (girl gangs) or famous figures (Camille Paglia).... *Tel 415/552–3034. 96 Lafayette St. between 11th and Howard Sts.; 26, 42 MUNI bus.*

The Marsh. The Monday night workshop performances at this Mission district performance-art petri dish are a good bet: See it here before it becomes the toast of off-off-Broadway.... *Tel 415/641–0235. 1062 Valencia St. at 22nd St.; 26 MUNI bus.*

Masonic Auditorium. Visiting symphonies and other classical artists appear in this large (3,165 seat), clean-lined hall booked by San Francisco Performances. You'll hear everything, but you might not see too much, due to unfortunate sight lines.... *Tel 415/776–4917. 1111 California St. between Taylor and Jones Sts.; California cable car; 1, 27 MUNI bus.*

Mission Cultural Center for Latino Arts. Works written and produced by multinational Latino artists are the *carne y papas* of this Mission district neighborhood center.... *Tel 415/821–1155. 2868 Mission St. between 24th and 25th Sts.; 24th St. BART/MUNI Metro stop; 14, 48 MUNI bus.*

New Langton Arts. Not afraid of controversy: Readings and performances at this on-the-edge nonprofit are often structured around a theme related to the art show in the site's gallery. Experimental fiction and minority voices get a fair hearing.... *Tel 415/626–5416. 1246 Folsom St. between 8th and 9th Sts.; 12, 19, 42 MUNI bus.*

Noe Valley Ministry. You never know what you might hear—chamber music, Celtic folk, straight-ahead jazz, punk thrash—at this eclectic room in the charming and quiet Noe Valley neighborhood.... *Tel 415/282–2317. 1021 Sanchez St. at 23rd St.; J Church streetcar; 24, 48 MUNI bus.*

Orpheum Theater. Touring shows—and the earthquake-displaced San Francisco Opera—find a temporary home in this 2,500-seat former vaudeville house.... *Tel 415/474–3800. 1192 Market St. near Civic Center; Civic Center BART/MUNI Metro stop; F streetcar; 5, 19, 37 MUNI bus.*

Palace of the Legion of Honor. The Florence Gould Auditorium in this Land's End landmark, newly reopened after its lengthy seismic retrofitting, makes a gorgeous, meditative backdrop for chamber music and organ recitals.... *Tel 415/750–3600. Lincoln Park, off Clement St. at 34th Ave., 18 MUNI bus.*

Punchline. Like Cobb's Comedy Club, the Punchline attracts nationally known comics; TV specials are occasionally taped here. Most nights feature a double or triple bill; Sundays spotlight local talent.... *Tel 415/397–7573. 444 Battery St. between Clay and Washington Sts., upstairs; California cable car; 1, 42 MUNI bus.*

The Red Vic Movie House. Special touches at this worker-owned-and-operated theater: Homemade cookies, bowls of popcorn with nutritional yeast, and cushy couches (in addition to ordinary movie seats). The brainy and underrated programming includes mini-festivals, recent American and European indie films, camp gems, boho favorites, and the occasional Hollywood classic.... *Tel 415/668–3994. 1727 Haight St. between Cole and Shrader Sts.; 6, 7, 37, 43, 66, 71 MUNI bus.*

The Roxie Cinema. Buy a big fat choco bar with a wrapper designed by R. Crumb, then enjoy the show at this Mission

SAN FRANCISCO ᗭ THE ARTS

flophouse cinema. Choose from: (a) obscure or classic film-noir gems; (b) contemporary Chinese action flicks; (c) new documentaries; or (d) retro pop treats. Sometimes the crowd can be a bit too knowing and ironic. Har-dee-har.... *Tel 415/863–1087. 16th St. at Valencia St.; 16th St. BART/MUNI Metro stop; 22, 26 MUNI bus.*

San Francisco Ballet. The first ballet company in the United States, and still one of the finest, under the hand of artistic director Helgi Tomasson. The eclectic programming offers something for everyone—even children.... *Tel 415/703–9400. Spring and fall seasons; performances at various venues.*

San Francisco Opera. Good luck getting tickets: The three-month (Sept–Dec) opera season is as sold solid as the 49ers. While the 1932 War Memorial Opera House is being retrofitted for earthquake safety and restored to its former opulence, the company is performing at various venues around town, including the recently restored (and renamed) Bill Graham Civic Auditorium.... *Tel 415/864–3330. War Memorial Opera House, 401 Van Ness Ave. near Grove St.; Van Ness, Civic Center BART/MUNI Metro stops; F streetcar; 5, 21, 42 MUNI bus.*

San Francisco Symphony. A new, hip, young (well, for classical music) conductor, Michael Tilson Thomas, left the London Symphony to revitalize this S.F. institution. Its huge, growing repertoire encompasses everything from classics to the avant garde, plus guest appearances by internationally known musicians and singers.... *Tel 415/431–5400. 201 Van Ness Ave. at Grove St.; Van Ness, Civic Center BART/MUNI Metro stops; F streetcar; 5, 21, 42 MUNI bus.*

S.F. Cinematheque. This 35-year-old avant-garde organization has around 70 screenings a year, and has supported such experimental pioneers as Stan Brakhage, Bruce Conner, Jonas Mekas, and the underground filmmaker everyone's heard of, Andy Warhol. Films here emphasize form rather than stories, and filmmakers are often on hand to talk about their wacky work.... *Tel 415/558–8129. 701 Mission St. at 3rd St.; 12, 26 MUNI bus (Thur). 800 Chestnut St. at Jones St.; Powell-Mason cable car; 15, 41 MUNI bus (Sun).*

Stage Door Theatre. Cabaret theater that hosts long runs of comedies and musical revues like John Fisher's outrageous, long-running *Medea: The Musical*.... *Tel 415/749–2228. 420 Mason St.; Powell-Mason cable car; 2, 3, 4, 76 MUNI bus.*

Survival Research Laboratories. Very underground, apparently allegorical spectacles, not designed to keep the fire marshal happy. Vintage S.R.L. shows involved mayhem by remote-controlled robots with dead animal parts, spewing flames and knives. If you can find a show, it's a once-in-a-lifetime experience by an artist and engineer many consider a genius.... *Web URL: http://www.srl.org.*

Theater Artaud. A contemporary space that takes a chance on premiering provocative, large-scale new dance and drama.... *Tel 415/621–7797. 460 Florida St. near 16th St.; 12, 22, 27, 33 MUNI bus.*

Theatre on the Square. Productions here are heavy on the music and dancing.... *Tel 415/433–9500. 450 Post St.; Powell BART/MUNI Metro stop; F streetcar; Powell-Hyde and Powell-Mason cable car; 2, 3, 4, 30, 45 MUNI bus.*

Theatre Rhinoceros. Sometimes original, sometimes retro, plays here are witty (or at least they think they are) and gay. Ditto the audience.... *Tel 415/861–5079. 2926 16th St. at South Van Ness Ave.; 16th St. BART/MUNI Metro stop; 22, 33, 53 MUNI bus.*

Total Mobile Home Micro Cinema. Cinema literally goes underground at this informal basement screening site. Programs frequently mix obscure old and new movies with live music and shenanigans. Xeroxed pamphlets provide instant film-history lessons.... *Tel 415/431–4007. 51 McCoppin St. off Valencia St.; F streetcar, 26 MUNI bus.*

spo

rts

When you mention sports in San Francisco, too many people think first of pitching rocks at riot police, sprinting away from the DEA through Golden Gate Park, or maybe some even more lurid, late-night examples of God-knows-who doing who-knows-what.

But for a place that could never be called sports-crazed, the greater Bay Area boasts an impressive lineup for fans: two of the most successful NFL clubs going, baseball teams of proud pedigree in both the American and National leagues, NHL and IHL hockey franchises, a Major League Soccer contender named after an angry British punk band, and something that at last report resembled an NBA franchise.

And when it comes to participatory sports, San Francisco truly leads the pack. Such sports as inline skating, Ultimate, and selling LSD at Grateful Dead concerts have either originated here or have been popularized here for national consumption. What'll be the next craze? Maybe a South American import called Futsal—soccer tailored for an indoor basketball court (see below)—but even San Franciscans still have to journey far afield to get in on the ground floor.

Sources
For spectator information on teams, games, times, locations, and broadcasts, check the San Francisco *Chronicle*'s daily "**Sporting Green**" section. The afternoon paper, the San Francisco *Examiner*, has an equally good stable of sportswriters and also provides information on spectator sports, but by the time you read this book—if rumors are to be believed—the *"Ex"* could be an ex-paper, due to a merger with the *"Chron."* The two papers together maintain a free **sports info line** (tel 415/808–5000, ext. 6000). Excellent play-by-play broadcasts, inane and inflammatory "Sports Talk" call-in commentary, and generally juicy gossip can be found on radio station **KNBR (680 AM)**.

How to Get Tickets
For sports tickets, the most convenient outlet is **BASS Tickets** (tel 510/762–BASS from San Francisco and the East Bay; 408/998–BASS from the South Bay), which will charge you about $3, if not more, for the pleasure of doing business. For Giants and Athletics games, dial the regular BASS numbers or their dedicated baseball line (tel 510/762–BALL). If you want to avoid the BASS surcharge, try the other numbers we list in the Lowdown. Suprisingly, there is no surcharge for Athletics games on Bass, only postage and handling.

The Lowdown

Where to watch

Pigskin... The scene at a **49ers** game is incalculably tamer than the atmosphere enjoyed by families attending Oakland Raiders games across the bay. For instance, though tattoos, body piercings, and the occasional shouting of obscenities are endured at windy, chilly **Candlestick Park** (now officially known by the locally despised tongue-twister "3-Com Park at Candlestick Point"), the pelting of fans wearing rival team colors with empty malt-liquor bottles is not. Still, don't spill your Candlestick chardonnay on the guy sitting below you when Jerry Rice catches a pass out of the slot and is kicking up the field's soggy sod on his way to the end zone.

The beloved 'Niners are always sold out, so tickets are hard to come by unless you know a season ticketholder who wants to unload some seats when a bad team is in town, or you're willing to pay scalpers a fool's ransom outside the park. Tip: the price scalpers charge for tickets is directly proportional to the quality of the visiting team—basic supply-and-demand stuff. For the extremely lucky, the 49ers put 700 tickets per game up for grabs every July on a first-come, first-serve basis over the telephone. Call the team's office at Candlestick (tel 415/468–2249) for more information.

Thrill seekers who do score 'Niners tickets can avoid paying the 'Stick's $20 charge for parking (it's $8 for baseball games) by leaving their cars in the down-in-the-mouth Hunters Point neighborhood behind Bret Harte Elementary School, located in back of the stadium. The area is definitely on the sketchy side, but once you pay approximately $5 to the entrepreneur who points you to a public curbside parking space, you and your car should be safe. Those who think about stiffing the "parking assistants" might be in for a surprise when they come back to their car: asked what the $5 parking charge is for, one of them growled, "Neighborhood watch," with neither a pause nor a smile.

Across the bay, the one-time bad boys of the NFL, the **Oakland Raiders**, play at the beautiful **Oakland–Alameda County Coliseum** (7000 Coliseum Way, Oakland). Although the foul-mouthed followers of the Silver and Black have a much-deserved reputation for rowdy, obnoxious, and sometimes violent behavior, it's worth the short trip from San Francisco to the coliseum on a BART train (Coliseum Station) to see the spectacle. Just make sure to wear black and keep your mouth shut if provoked. Tickets to individual games are sometimes available through the **Oakland Football Marketing Association** (tel 510/615–1875).

Peanuts and Cracker Jack... The **San Francisco Giants** (tel 415/467–8000) field two of the major league's most powerful bats in Barry Bonds and Matt Williams, but fans of big-league pitching duels too often see the team's spotty pitching staff fall on their own swords before the seventh-inning stretch at **Candlestick**. If you want to see the "sophisticated" S.F. baseball crowd turn ugly, your best bet is to coordinate your visit with the Los Angeles Dodgers, who are hated here even though (or maybe because) the rivalry hardly raises the finely plucked eyebrows of jaded fans in the Southland. Come the year 2000, the Giants are scheduled to move into a state-of-the-art stadium in China Basin (home runs hit over the right-field fence will plop down in San Francisco Bay!), but until then, bundle up to catch S.F.'s boys of summer braving the 'Stick's cruel, bone-chilling winds. Giants' tickets are available through BASS, as well as at any of five Giants Dugout stores in the Bay Area or in person at the San Francisco Giants ticket office (at Candlestick, Gate B; Mon–Fri 8:30–5, Sat–Sun during home games, 8:30am–end of game).

The setting across the bay at an **Oakland A's** (tel 510/638–0500) game is much more pastoral, and always warmer. Though efforts to placate Raiders owner Al Davis have grafted retractable seating and luxury suites where the beloved bleachers used to be, the **Coliseum** is still one of the most enjoyable places in the country to watch a baseball game. The mainly blue-collar, family-for-tified crowd minds its manners but knows how to have a good time, so grab a beer and a Coliseum Dog and wait for A's slugger Mark McGwire to park one in those new sun-drenched retractable outfield seats (yuck!). That is, if the A's decide not to pack their bats and leave for another city. The Oakland A's ticket office is at the Coliseum (near Gate D, Mon–Fri 9–6, Sat 10–4).

Slapshots... The pride of the South Bay, the NHL's **San Jose Sharks**, entertain their enthusiastic fans between Zamboni passes at the recently built **San Jose Arena** (525 W. Santa Clara St., San Jose). The team skates from October to May and was a credible Stanley Cup con-tender from 1993 to '95, though it has fallen on hard times recently. Call 408/287–9200 for game information; for individual tickets, contact BASS.

Hoop dreams... During the 1996–97 season, the NBA's **Golden State Warriors**, the perennial Team of the Future, will play roundball at the **San Jose Arena** while the **Oakland Coliseum Arena**—adjacent to the Oakland–Alameda County Coliseum—undergoes renovations. The Warriors' season starts in November and ends, not coinci-dentally, when the NBA playoffs begin in April. Warriors fans at the Coliseum were generally well-behaved and enthusiastic, and there's no reason for that to change in "Anything to Please" San Jose. Call 510/986–2200 for game information; for individual tickets, contact BASS.

Should I stay or should I goal?... Also in the South Bay is the well-received Major League Soccer club the **San Jose Clash**, who play from April to September at downtown S.J.'s **Spartan Stadium**. Because of its 30,000-plus capacity, the erstwhile home of San Jose State Spartan football usually has tickets to spare for soccer matches, and seats start at a paltry $7. Though profes-sional soccer in the U.S. traditionally has been kicked around like Dick Nixon, the Clash draw a healthy crowd that includes large contingents of the area's soccer-fanatic Hispanic population and wide-eyed youngsters who play the game themselves. Call 408/241–9922 for game infor-mation; for individual tickets, contact BASS or the Spartan Stadium Box Office (tel 408/924–6333; 290 South 7th St., San Jose).

SAN FRANCISCO $\smile$ SPORTS

The ponies... You can play the ponies at two tracks in the Bay Area. The East Bay's **Golden Gate Fields** (tel 510/559–7300; 110 Eastshore Hwy., Albany), right outside Berkeley, has races from December to mid-June, with off-track betting year-round. Admission starts at $3. **Bay Meadows** (tel 415/574–7223; 2600 S. Delaware St., San Mateo), which is accessible from San Francisco by rail on CalTrain, offers free live entertainment like country-and-western bands Fridays, as well as $1 beers and hot dogs. The season runs from September to April.

Drag, the hetero way... The action is fast, furious, and at times a bit ridiculous at **Sears Point International Raceway** (tel 800/870–RACE; at the junction of routes 37 and 121 in Sonoma) during Wednesday Night Drags, where everything from dragsters to Volkswagen Beetles and all manner of souped-up station wagons compete in amateur drag races. From 4 till 10pm, February through November (unless it's raining), up to 300 cars and motorcycles race against the clock. Admission is $10; participants pay just $17, but you'll need a valid driver's license and your car will be subject to a safety check. (It's probably not a good idea to pull your rental car up to the line.)

Where to play

Anarchy on wheels... Agro-bike messengers festooned with all manner of body art unite with other pissed-off pedal-pushers to take over the city streets during **Critical Mass** on the last Friday of every month. If you're feeling frisky, just do as the locals do and berate red-faced motorists from your bicycle. The action starts at **Justin Herman Plaza** at or around 5:30 or 6pm and follows a route that changes every time so the group can run—or pedal—afoul of authorities, who begrudgingly accept the demonstration-like event. Recent rides have traveled to Candlestick Park for a Giants game and to Marin County for camping. Organizers advise potential participants to come with their own bicycle and bring a festive attitude. Critical Mass operates on many philosophical levels, with some riders joining in to protest the car culture, some to make other political statements, and some just to prove that up to 2,000 people can organize an event that runs itself. The ride is usually over by 7pm, according to the San Francisco Bicycle Coalition (tel 415/431–2453), which stresses that neither it nor any other group "organizes" the event.

Son of anarchy on wheels... Almost measuring up to the spectacle provided by Critical Mass, albeit a tad less political and more well-scrubbed, are **The Midnight Rollers**. This roller-skating, hard-partying herd of up to 700 starts its shimmy at 8pm every Friday evening at a parking lot across from the Ferry Building at the foot of Market Street. From there the raucous throng rolls to Pier 39, Aquatic Park, Fort Mason, the Marina Green, the Palace of Fine Arts (where they hold hands and snake through the landmark's illuminated courtyards), Chinatown, and Union Square, down the Powell Street cablecar line, through SOMA, up the Embarcadero, and back to the Ferry Building, where they party in the parking lot. This very inclusive free event—even bicyclists and joggers are welcome—can take 3 hours or longer, depending on the number of bars the group visits on any given run. It's advisable to bring along blinking lights, light sticks, and a helmet, all of which organizers sell at a nominal cost, and do try to avoid the potentially deadly train tracks running down many streets. For the latest information on the event, call **D.M.J. Inline Sports Marketing** (tel 415/753–1967).

Inline hockey... Gluttons for punishment can strap on their skates for pick-up inline hockey games and league play at China Basin's **Bladium** (tel 415/442–5060; 1050 3rd St.). Afternoon pick-up games are played seven days a week, but hour-and-a-half late-night matches are enjoined only on Sunday at 10pm. The owners provide all equipment, including helmet, shin guards, stick, gloves, elbow pads, and skates, for a $10 rental fee. The action is limited to 16 players, so show up early because it usually fills up. The cost to play is $10 for non-members ($8 for members, who also pay a $35 yearly fee), but goalies play for free (not including equipment rental) because "that's the only way to get 'em," according to the rink's owners.

Camping out... As far as camping in San Francisco goes, the pickings are slim. But one terrific location is **Angel Island** in the middle of San Francisco Bay. Angel Island has nine "environmental camping" spots—meaning no wood fires and an "if you carry it in, you carry it out" trash policy—that afford great views of San Francisco, Oakland, or Marin. You can bring camp stoves or barbecue coals, but be prepared to lug all supplies up to two miles to the various sites, which include pit toilets and water. The island, which bears the ignominy of having hosted a detention camp for Chinese immigrants in the early-to-middle part of the century, is choked with eucalyptus and lilac trees and features the 781-foot Mount Livermore. After a long hike up paved but untrafficked roads to the summit, hikers are usually blessed with a completely fogged-in view. Also on the island is a pleasant bay where the Red and White Fleet ferry (tel 415/546–2896, 415/546–2700; round trip is $10 for adults; ferries depart Mon–Fri 10am, weekends 10, 12pm, and 2) docks after its short trip from San Francisco's Pier 43½. The camping spots fill up very quickly, so it's advisable to make reservations the maximum six months in advance. Each spot costs $7 to $9 per night, depending on the season, and can be booked through a company in San Diego named **Destinet** (tel 800/444–PARK); more information on ferry schedules and special events is available through the rangers office (tel 415/435–1915).

Ultimate... Developed in the late 1970s and still gaining in worldwide popularity, Wham-O's favorite hybrid of football, soccer, and toy-tossing is played on Tuesday and Thursday nights at Sharon Meadow (a.k.a. "Hippy Hill") in **Golden Gate Park** near the Haight. Walk-ons are welcome at the free pick-up games, which start at 6:30pm, and the regulars—whom one player describes as "an eclectic mix of computer nerds and ex-Deadheads, ranging in age from 21 to 35"—are easygoing and will gladly teach newcomers the finer points of the game.

There's a winter league in **Jackson Playground** (in Potrero Hill at 17th St. and Arkansas St.) that plays evening games from November through March, but those who want to slog it out on the park's often muddy field must pony up $50 for the season, which includes a post-season party. "Party" is a word that comes up often in the world of San Francisco Ultimate, and the players, some of whom brew their own beer and smoke more grass than they kick up with their cleats—are known to throw some wild ones. The **San Francisco Ultimate Club** has a local phone number that mysteriously gets disconnected every summer; at last report it was 415/522–SFUC. Information on ultimate frisbee tournaments and related topics can be found on the World Wide Web under the query "ultimate frisbee" or "frisbee sports."

What a racket... For information on any of city's 69 free tennis courts—21 of which are lighted—call the **Recreation and Parks Department** at 415/753–7100. **Mission Dolores Park** (Dolores St. at 18th St.) has six lighted tennis courts that are open until 10:45 every night. Since the park is a popular business address for a wide range of drug dealers, be careful at night: If someone mutters "chiba" in your direction, keep on walking, unless of course you want to be loose—real loose—for the big match. Dropping by a private tennis club for a few quick volleys in S.F. can be difficult, because few of them offer limited-time memberships. If you're staying at the Marriott, however, perhaps the best club in town, the **San Francisco Tennis Club** (tel 415/777–9000; 645 5th St.) is at your disposal several blocks away. A four-level structure complete with a snack bar, the Tennis Club has something for everybody, even those of you who hate tennis: 12 indoor courts, 16 outdoor courts, USPTA-certified pros, basketball, free weights, martial arts, yoga, volleyball, and child care. It stays open until 10:30 weeknights and until 7 on weekends; court time costs $10 per hour before 4pm, $20 after. The **San Francisco Bay Club** (tel 415/433–2550 or 2200; 150 Greenwich St.) can arrange for a one-week pass to its 75,000-square-foot space, the largest in San Francisco, including racquetball and squash courts as well as two rooftop tennis courts. The club stays open until 11 weeknights, until 9 weekends.

The **Mission Recreation Center** (tel 415/695–5012; 2450 Harrison) keeps its two racquetball courts open until the center's 9:30 closing on weekday nights (it closes at 4:30pm on Saturday and at 5 on Sunday) They're available on a first-come, first-serve basis for a half-hour at a time. The center also has ping-pong tables, but if you lose a ball, you're gonna cough up 25 cents, bud.

Volleyball... If you have your own net and ball, go to **Moscone Playground** (1800 Chestnut St., in the Marina District), where the lights stay on at night for baseball leagues Monday to Friday, March to October. You might also find informal, pick-up action on the western part of the nearby Marina Green (no lights here, though). **Kezar Pavilion** (tel 415/753–7032; Stanyan St. at Waller St.) has a drop-in volleyball program that operates year-round except during September. The pavilion has two courts, one for men only and one for co-ed play. The program runs from 7 to 9:30pm on Mondays, and also on Tuesdays from mid-June until September. The cost to get into a game is $2.

Fore!... If therapy for you means smacking the skin off a few dozen golf balls at a driving range, you have two night-time options in the S.F. area. In 3 years, **Mission Bay Golf** (tel 415/431–7888; 1200 6th St. at Channel St.) has burned itself in the subconscious of many a San Franciscan due to its location almost under Highway 280 in Mission Bay. If motorists on this usually uncongested stretch of raised asphalt look down at just the right time, they will almost be blinded by the facility's high-intensity floodlights. Mission Bay Golf's 66 stalls, crammed onto two tiers, are open until 11pm seven days a week. Also on site are a chipping area, putting green, restaurant, pro shop, and professional instructors. A bucket of balls costs $7. The other illuminated tees in the area belong to a more evocatively named enterprise, **El Camino Driving Range**, which is located in South San Francisco (tel 415/583–9696; 1095 Mission Rd. at Grant Ave.). Its 19 stalls are also open until 11 every night, and 110 balls cost $7.

Futsal, anyone?... One of the newest sporting activities gaining popularity in San Francisco is Futsal, which was originally made popular by professional soccer stars in South America and has been introduced locally by Brazilians living in the Bay Area. Basically, the game can be described as soccer on a basketball court, only the ball is much smaller and heavier so it won't bounce out of play as often, and there are five players per side. At each end of the court are goals that are similar to, if a bit larger than, the goals used in lacrosse. Because of the high-speed nature of the game, it helps soccer players develop ball-handling skills. Though the game is played Wednesday nights after 10 at the **Boys Club** on Paige and Stanyan, the competition there is strictly a league affair. The league's good-natured organizers do welcome visitors to stop by and check it out, however. To get into a Futsal game, you have to drive almost an hour down the peninsula to Mountain View, where **Foothill College** has a program on Monday nights starting at 10.

Climb any mountain... Agoraphobes can find solace at **Mission Cliffs** (tel 415/550–0515; 2295 Harrison St. off 19th St.), a Mission District indoor rock-climbing center that boasts 14,000 square feet of sculpted climbing walls up to 50 feet high. Mission Cliffs, also popular with social climbers, offers beginners an introductory package that includes a day pass ($12), equipment rental ($6), and an hour-long lesson ($5). The Cliffs are open until 10pm Monday through Friday (when the last introductory class starts at 7:30), and until 6pm on weekends. On the first Friday of every month, from 5pm until closing, women climbers pay half price on everything—lessons, rental, admission—except retail goods.

Bowling for cocktails... The sport of Middle America, in all its polyester and scuffed-leather glory, takes a turn for the hip in the Haight at **Park Bowl**, a k a "Rock 'n' Bowl" (tel 415/752–2366; 1855 Haight St.), where the white-trash aesthetic is currently riding a fashion wave. On Thursday, Friday, and Saturday nights, this neighborhood institution, located a block from Golden Gate Park, combines bowling with rock videos or a live deejay until 2 in the morning. And the place serves cheap drinks, too. But catch it while you can, because there's a rumor floating around that a record store may soon take over this old-school alley. **Japantown Bowl** (tel 415/921–6200; Post St. at Webster St.) keeps the pins flying 24 hours a day in a somewhat sterile and completely computerized atmosphere. This is a good bet for redemption after you bomb out at any of Japantown's many karaoke bars.

For gym rats... If you drank too much espresso during the day and can't get to sleep, what better way to work off the 2am demons than hitting the weights? Although **24-Hour Nautilus** (tel 415/776–2200; 1200 Van Ness Ave. at Post St.) doesn't quite live up to its name—it closes at midnight on Fridays, at 10pm Saturdays, and at 8pm Sundays—it may be the last hope for insomniacs. It's got all weight and cardio machines you need, plus free weights, an aerobics studio, sauna, and jacuzzi, and it costs

SAN FRANCISCO ⟨ SPORTS

$15 a day for non-members. **Gold's Gym** has one branch in town (tel 415/626–8865; 333 Valencia St. at 14th St.); it stays open until 11 weeknights and 8 weekends, and for a $10 day pass you get your basic, no-nonsense weights and machines. The 10-floor YMCA downtown (tel 415/885–0460; 220 Golden Gate Ave. at Leavenworth St.) leaves other by-night work-out options in the dust, with free weights, Universal, Nautilus, indoor walking and running tracks, a swimming pool, a basketball court, two racquetball courts, a boxing room with punching bags and mirrors, a rooftop sun deck and garden, two aerobics studios, a cafe, and massage service. Come here for a slice of San Francisco. Open until 10 weeknights and Saturdays and until 7 Sundays.

Gone fishin'... For good night fishing, head to **Ocean Beach**, located on the Great Highway at the extreme west end of the city, just south of the Golden Gate and the famous Cliff House. Surf-casting abounds all the way down to **Half Moon Bay**, about 30 miles from the city. (A good spot in between is **Rockaway Beach** in Pacifica, about 15 miles south of S.F.) Though at various times of the year these coastal waters are patrolled by perch, kingfish, and sharks, it's mainly the striped bass that run at night, out beyond the breakers. You'll need at least an 11- or 12-foot rod, 17-pound line, a 3-ounce sinker, a good lure, and either an annual ($15.20) or one-day ($5) ocean fishing license. Licenses and supplies are available at a variety of S.F. fishing stores, but a good bet is **G&M Sales Co.** (tel 415/863–2855; 1667 Market St.), an outdoors outfitter in the middle of the city. The guys working the fishing department can fill you in on where the stripers are running and outfit you for the job. If you choose Ocean Beach, don't be surprised to find company: many people build fires and party there, especially under the light of a full moon, and the crowds are usually very social.

Rack 'em, Dano... As a faithful reader of *Billiards Digest*, you probably already know that the magazine's editors recently rated **Chalkers Billiard Club** (tel 415/512–0450; in the Rincon Center, 101 Spear St.; open until 2am, until 11pm Sun) as the number-two billiard room in the nation. It has going for it 30 custom-made cherrywood tables, a full bar that overlooks the playing area, a kitchen, a pro shop, and a decidedly elegant atmosphere, with dozens of fine oil paintings on the walls and parchment lampshades on the custom-made light fixtures. Because of its Financial District location, Chalkers attracts a young, white-collar crowd that often pops in before or after hitting the fine restaurants or nightclubs in the area. Evening rates start at $10 an hour for two people, $12 an hour on weekends. **South Beach Billiards** (tel 415/495–5939; 270 Brannon St.; open until 2am) has a slightly hipper crowd than its Financial District competitor due to its location near South Park, a k a "Goatee Gulch," the center of the wired world. South Beach has a full bar and cafe, 36 regulation tables, one snooker table, and the only indoor bocce court in northern California. Per-table rates here are $12 an hour on weeknights, $15 an hour on weekends.

The oldest pool hall in the city stands like a shrine to the game in the seediest part of town, the Tenderloin. Though the name has changed over the years, **Hollywood Billiards** (tel 415/252–9643; 61 Golden Gate Ave.) dates to the turn of the century, and the atmosphere is straight out of the movies: you almost expect to see Minnesota Fats or Willie Moscone running one of its 37 antique tables. Open 24 hours a day, the hall also features a snooker table, a billiards table, two 5-by-10-foot tables, dart boards, video games, an impressive selection on the jukebox, and a kitchen that churns out sandwiches, nachos, and chili. Although the club is highly recommended, and really a must-see for fans of old-style billiards, the neighborhood is such that you should take advantage of the hall's valet parking if you decide to drive there. Just outside is notorious 6th Street, with its pungent collection of winos and sex joints, and the Jones Street and Taylor Street sides feature more of the same, always ready to satisfy your cravings for late-night tattoos, bad wine, or simply a piss in the street.

The most popular pool joint with kiddies is **The Great Entertainer** (tel 415/861–8833; 975 Bryant St.— one block from the Hall of Justice!), whose cheesy, food-like restaurant fare allows it to skate past a city ordinance barring those under age 18 from pool halls. After 8 on Fridays and Saturdays, however, no one under 21 is allowed in unless accompanied by a parent. Besides pastel colors, The Great Entertainer also features 42 tables, darts, a ping-pong table, and video games.

hangi

ng out

Hanging out is an officially sanctioned activity in San Francisco. Although many people here do hold down jobs to support their relaxation habits, this place is utterly unlike certain other type-A cities, which will go unmentioned. Night and day, you'll find lots of company and support here for your lack of ambition and drive—there are lots of other folks around who are quite visibly and happily going nowhere in particular, and are in no hurry at all to get there. Legendary home of those ancient no-work and all-play tribes called the Beats and the Hippies, San Francisco is the birthplace of Slack.

The city's ludicrously plentiful and idiosyncratic cafes are, of course, the most obvious resort for hanging out; there's at least one of these caffeinated hangout havens open late in every neighborhood, and people use them as they would their own living rooms. (See The Cafe Scene.) And late-night shops like Tower Records and the Virgin Megastore are another good destination, when you just want to hear some music, browse through some magazines, and watch some people.

But there are all sorts of ways to hang out, and all levels, from slacker subsistence to swellegant. By definition, hanging out doesn't require much money, but that shouldn't keep you from hanging among the rich and famous. In fact, that's one of the most amusing (and challenging) ways to hang. Hotel lobbies and fancy hotel bars are good spots for nursing a single drink or a cup of coffee or tea as you look, listen, eavesdrop, fantasize about what other people are up to, judge them mercilessly, and ultimately be glad for your own life. Sweet spots for observing the rich and the wanna-be rich are The Compass Rose, on the mezzanine level of the St. Francis Hotel at Union Square, with its antiques, eccentric furniture, $60 glasses of port (and thankfully, $2 pots of tea), and the Art Deco Redwood Room in the landmark Four Seasons Clift Hotel, with its carved redwood panels, Klimt prints, soft piano music, nice cocktails and snacks, and friendly bartenders who will watch out for a woman alone. The Youth Hostel at Fort Mason is another good, free hangout: You can sink into the soft couches in front of the ever-burning fireplace and eavesdrop on foreign travelers to your heart's content—it's like traveling without ever leaving. You get the idea. Use your imagination. You can do nothing, and spend nothing, just about anywhere here.

Yes, the entire city of San Francisco is a loafer's paradise, but some areas are more hospitable and interesting than others. Here's an aerial view of the city's neighborhoods, listed in descending order of hangability.

The **Haight** *was* The Summer of Love, and the neighborhood will never get the tie-dye and hash residue out of its system. There are really two Haights: In the **Lower Haight**, you get grungy and share attitude problems with the burnouts, skinheads, and skate rats; in the **Upper Haight**, you spend cash and window-shop among same. The **Mission** is a true melting pot, where spiffily-dressed, lively Latinos mix with lazy, thrift-shop clad slackers and anxiously slumming yuppies looking for the trendiest new clubs and restaurants. See it now: This vivid neighborhood, with its mix of the beautiful and the horrible, the rich and the unspeakably poor, is unavoidably headed for gentrification and its attendant loss of character.

The **Castro**, epicenter of the Queer Nation (the gay/lesbian/bi/transgender movement), is a totally gay neighborhood, with an exuberant street life with junk food joints, all night cafes, a 24-hour Walgreens, and bars, bars, bars, spilling open to the street. **Cow Hollow** is the straight yuppie playground and would be the hetero equivalent of the Castro if straight people needed a place they could feel safe among their own: meat market bars, trendy restaurants, and pricey boutiques galore. **South of Market**, also known as SOMA, only comes out at night. With its wide, flat streets near old piers, SOMA is the closest you'll get to Manhattan on the West Coast. When the lights go off in this warehouse and discount shopping district, the lights go on in clubs, loft theaters, and restaurants. The leathermen head for the Folsom Street bars, while the club kids scatter to the disco, punk, and alternative clubs tucked into warehouses.

North Beach is an Italian theme park bordering **Chinatown**, full of charming boutiques, boisterous bars, and glowing family-run cafes. **Pacific Heights** is a postcard-pretty village on a hill above the Marina, with safe streets, good window shopping and restaurants, and so clean and tidy you'll feel like you have to take your shoes off. **Noe Valley** is a calm, family-style neighborhood full of middle-aged professionals who finally gave up on living the Mission, Haight, or Castro high life, but 24th Street is a sweet, safe stroll with good window-shopping and restaurants. The Richmond and the Sunset are called the **Avenues**, and they're essentially in-city suburbs, without much nightlife to speak of. But they're near **Ocean Beach** and **Golden Gate Park**, which are great for nighttime walks. And last, is the notorious **Tenderloin**, a strictly at-your-own-risk district of high-density urban blight, which offers drive-by shootings, peep shows and $25 blow jobs, easily obtainable crack and crystal, and cheap restaurants.

That said, we have to note that S.F. is not a 24-hour town—but if you know where to look, you can find whatever you want or need.

The Lowdown

Tattoo you... You don't want to leave San Francisco with just another Hard Rock Cafe T-shirt, a Golden Gate fog-dome, or a loaf of sourdough from the airport gift shop, do you? No. The most authentic (and longest-lasting!) S.F. souvenir is a new tattoo or body-piercing. And, perhaps because of its deliciously sinful, seedy, sailor-filled history, the city has more tattoo shops per capita than any other U.S. metropolis. Getting a tattoo is an after-dark sort of thing, usually after you've had a few (judgment-altering substances, that is). And though the business has cleaned up its act, given its newfound popularity and attendant government scrutiny, it may never be a nine-to-five sort of thing, so "office hours" often vary according to the whims, moods, and lifestyles of the skin artists.

Start in North Beach at **Lyle Tuttle Tattoo Studio, Museum & Gallery** (tel 415/775–4991; 841 Columbus Ave. near Lombard St.; open daily till 8; Fri, Sat till 10) How do you put a tattoo on display? Ask Tuttle, the grand marshal of this nonstop skin parade, or his assistant, Krystyne the Kolorful, both of whom do on-premises tattooing. "Until 1905, tattooing was a slow and painful process," they assure us. "With the invention of the Electric Tattooing Machine, the average design may be completed in a matter of minutes, with the benefit of hospital-type sterilization." Hmmm. Well, we'll walk around a bit and think about it.

Next stop in North Beach is a visit with famous skin artist Ed Hardy at his **Tattoo City** (tel 415/433–9437; 722 Columbus Ave.; open nightly till 8).

Hardy is considered one of the best in the country, and one of his specialties is "cover-up art"—taking an unwanted tattoo (for instance, that gaudy "So-and-So Forever" you had etched over your heart just a week before the breakup) and turning it into something you can live with—names of outdated lovers become roses, and so forth. At **Anubis Warpus** (tel 415/431–2218; 1525 Haight St.; open nightly till 8), you can buy a book on the history of tattoos (from a startling array of books and magazines all radiating a fashionably bad attitude), then tromp your Doc Martens to the back of the shop and have your favorite design permanently inked by the resident skin artist. Other reputable and well-established skin joints include **Gauntlet** (tel 415/431–3133; 2377 Market St. near Castro St.) and **Body Manipulations** (tel 415/621–0408; 254 Fillmore St. at Haight St.).

Best window-shopping... Night and day, San Francisco's window-shopping and materialistic Wishful-thinking Central is the relentlessly upscale **Union Square**, the city's fanciest and most famous shopping district, and the unofficial city center. At night, the 2.6-acre park is a haven for drifters and street people, and should probably be avoided, but it's fun to browse the brightly lit windows of the tony shops on the bordering streets, including Chanel; Tiffany & Co.; Armani; Neiman Marcus; Macy's; Saks Fifth Avenue; Lord & Taylor; Hermès; Cartier; and the local emporium, Gumps. A side street called Maiden Lane, which housed bordellos at the turn of the century, is now a quaint, car-free cluster of chic cafes and boutiques, and features Frank Lloyd Wright's 1948 Circle Gallery Building, a prototype for Manhattan's Guggenheim Museum. Our favorite window-shopping experience is the Sanrio superstore (39 Stockton St.), three-story home of Hello Kitty and her cute friends. Since the 19th century, the six-block stretch of Union Street from Gough to Steiner, now nicknamed **Cow Hollow,** has gone from grazing pasture to browsing haven—its remodeled Victorians now house hip and haute boutiques and galleries, cafes and restaurants—but you can still spot warmblooded mammals ambling by as they ponder if the grass is greener on the other side of the street. Cow Hollow is rivaled by **Fillmore Street**, between Jackson and Geary, which has undergone its own evolution, from a neglected and faintly dangerous area into a five-block strip of chic boutiques (Mike for sleek, stylized home furnishings and Fillamento for beautiful things you don't really need) and trendy restaurants (Elite Café, Mozzarella da Buffalo,

Pauli's Café). The superfancy **Jackson Square** area, bounded by Montgomery and Sansome, Jackson and Washington streets, is now the city's glittering antiques treasure trove and showroom center for fabric and furniture. The city's first designated historic district, Jackson Square contains the only group of downtown buildings that survived the 1906 quake and fire.

Chinatown, home to some 200,000 Chinese-Americans, (making it the second-largest Chinese community in the U.S. behind New York), is bustling and busy and always intriguing late into the night. Don't even think of driving down crowded, congested main tourist streets Grant and Stockton (between Bush St. and Broadway). Besides, Chinatown is best experienced on foot—you'd miss all the sights, sounds, tastes, and especially smells of these streets and their innumerable little side alleys, souvenir shops, and groceries. You might consider **Castro Street** (between Market St. and 20th St.) the mecca of San Francisco's gay and lesbian population. Aside from the multitude of buzzing, booming bars, most of which are open to the street so you can browse the patrons (and vice versa), this lively-till-late thoroughfare bustles with pizza joints, bars, cafes, and juice bars, ravewear boutiques, and the institution called Cliff's Variety, one of the most unusual hardware stores in the country, which always has a hilariously campy display—like a mannequin soap opera or an appliance pageant—in the window. Over the hill from the Castro is the time warp known as **Haight Street**, which is lined from Masonic to Stanyan with cafes and restaurants; head shops; alternative book, record, food, and clothing boutiques; and more vintage clothing shops than anywhere else in this retro-crazed city. A magnet for hippie hold-outs, skate rats, runaways, panhandlers, skinheads, dealers, and what-have-you, the Haight can be a little sinister after dark, so use common sense when walking here.

Browsing for books... Sure, reading is traditionally a solitary pastime, but after the sun sets, Bay Area bookworms gravitate toward the city's abundant, unusual, and personality-filled bookstores, looking for literate, like-minded companions, as well as new brain candy. Many of San Francisco's best bookstores keep late hours for restless readers. And yes, coffee can usually be found on the premises, or nearby. The Mission district's **Abandoned Planet** (tel 415/861–4695; 518 Valencia St. near 16th St.; open daily until 11) specializes in literature, art, Spanish, photography, Beat writers, and with its cozy window seats and couches (you may have to convince one of the shop's several cats to share one with you), it's a comforting, low-key evening hangout. **A Different Light**, in the Castro, (tel 415/431–0891; 489 Castro St. at 18th St.; open daily till 11) is sort of the Library of Congress of the West Coast's largest gay community, functioning as a community center and meeting place, as well as a book mecca. Among the large selection of gay and lesbian books and magazines, you'll find handmade fanzines, community newspapers, and event fliers. The shop also hosts readings and signings for gay and lesbian writers ranging from Olympic swimmer Greg Louganis to tennis star–cum–mystery novelist Martina Navratilova. With a name taken from Hemingway, **A Clean, Well-Lighted Place for Books** (tel 415/441–6670; Van Ness Ave. at Golden Gate Ave.; open Fri, Sat till midnight) attracts yupscale customers who work and soak up the arts in the culture-rich Civic Center neighborhood (Davies Symphony Hall and the War Memorial Opera House are just down the street). Lots of table displays and stools encourage browsing—and mingling—and the variety of titles is exceptional. Just for the contrast and the cranky, character-filled cavernousness of it, we also like downtown's **McDonald's Book Shop** (tel 415/673–2235; 48 Turk St.; open daily till 11 or so) which calls itself "a dirty, poorly lit place for books." Who knows what (or who) you'll unearth among the heaps of books, magazines, and records in this perpetual rummage sale. If you're lucky (and if you're not too proud or embarrassed to ask), aging Beat poet Lawrence Ferlinghetti may pose for a picture with you in front of the legendary **City Lights Bookstore** (tel 415/362–8193; 261 Columbus Ave.; open daily till 11), Beat headquarters in North Beach. Yes, Jack Kerouac and Allen Ginsberg were here, and poet and founder Ferlinghetti is still hanging around. City Lights could easily rest on its laurels; instead, the enterprise keeps current by publishing a wide range of literary classics and experimental books and by stocking an amazing array of handmade art books and quirky zines in the mind-altering consignment section in the main floor's back room. Not so coincidentally, two history-encrusted (or just crusty) North Beach beatnik bars of yore, **Spec's** and **Vesuvios**, are located a shot glass's throw away, and both of them will inspire a poem or at least a page in your journal. If you like your bookstores big and messy, look no further than Richmond district's **Green Apple Books** (tel 415/387–2272; 506 Clement St.; open daily till 11). Two stories crammed to the ceiling with musty old tomes (and a few new ones), this wooden maze is a fire hazard, and an instant death site should an earthquake hit. But it's worth the risk for bibliomaniacs, who come for S.F.'s largest selection of used books. The salesclerks often lead bewildered shoppers by the hand to sections, because verbal directions are impossible. But there's treasure amid the chaos: San Franciscans have repeatedly named this their favorite bookstore, mostly because bargains and rare titles await discovery. Scope out the crazy array of masks on display and the excellent art section, the graphic-novel selection (ask for a clerk named Ivan) and the pulp and rare fiction (ask for Kevin). **Borders Books and Music** (tel 415/399–1633; 400 Powell St. at Post St.; open daily till 11) is anything but dispossessed. A Union Square superstore and part of a national chain, it's clean, organized, and always busy. The selection is enormous—you can spend hours browsing here—and its newsstand is the best in the city. There are lots of chairs and reading nooks, and you can drag your pile of new reads into the on-premises cafe.

If you'd rather look at famous writers than read their work, a good bet is the **Hayes Street Grill** (tel 415/863–5545; 320 Hayes St.), before or after one of the frequent City Arts and Lectures events at nearby **Herbst Theater** (call 415/392–4400 for a schedule).

Browsing for newspapers and magazines... As we said earlier, **Borders** takes the honors as the city's top newsstand, thanks to its broad collection of general, international, and even alternative titles, but sometimes you want more surprises. If any store brings together every trait of the Haight, that nexus of booze, drugs, creative panhandling, piercing, tats and alt.everything in general, it would be **Naked Eye News & Video** (tel 415/864–2985; 533 Haight St.; open daily till 11), which stocks an eye-popping array of publications, from mainstream dailies, newsmagazines, and computer rags to obscure fetish journals and zines celebrating drugs, skateboards, self-described fat dykes, and transsexuals (sometimes all at once). And then there's the video-for-rent selection. **The Magazine** (tel 415/441–7731; 920 Larkin St. between Post and Geary Sts.; open daily till 10) is where old magazines go to die. All those old hot-rod magazines and *National Geographic*s that used to be in your attic and basement have somehow found their way into the stacks at the front of this Tenderloin store. But the action is in the back of the shop, where you'll discover The Magazine's raison d'être: ancient porn, both straight and gay, and all obsessively catalogued. This area is populated almost exclusively by guys hunting for that first issue of *Playboy* (or *Playgirl*) they discovered in Dad's sock drawer.

Dressing for sexcess... Sometimes even adults need toys to play with, with friends or alone. The user-friendly, nonfurtive specialty shop **Good Vibrations** (tel 415/974–8980; 1210 Valencia St. at 21st; open daily till 8) is nationally known for its outstanding vibrator collection— and its Vibrator Museum, a gathering of dildos through the ages, from the standard latex-reeking, flesh-colored facsimile to dolphin-shaped models for women who don't even want to think about men. Though this Mission district shop is owned and run by lesbians, the awesome array of products caters to all sexual tastes—evolved men are welcome too. There's also an extensive collection of how-to (and do-it-yourself) books on everybody's favorite subject. A Castro neighborhood shop called **Jaguar** (tel 415/863–4777; 4057 18th St. near Castro St.; open daily till midnight) also carries a dazzling array of erotica and sexual supplies, theirs of the men-on-men variety.

Groceries after hours... Eating late doesn't mean you have to be at the mercy of junk-food chains. Go shopping instead, and bring your feast home, or have a midnight picnic at one of the many scenic, outdoor nightspots mentioned later in this chapter. **Harvest Ranch Market** (tel 415/626–0805; 2285 Market St. at 16th St.; open daily till 11), is a gourmet grocery in the Castro, with an enormous and gorgeous spread of soups and salad-makings, plus sandwiches, cheeses, juices, snacks, rustic benches out front, and always a gaggle of interesting-looking people and interesting-looking dogs. There are always the two **Safeway** markets, all-night grocery stores with distinctive personalities. The **Marina Safeway** (tel 415/563–4946; 15 Marina Blvd.) is a famous straight pickup scene, immortalized in *Tales of the City,* Armistead Maupin's serialized novel of S.F. You might meet your sweetie (or just tonight's fast-food passion) in the aisles or checkout line. Across town, near the Castro, the **Market Street Safeway** (tel 415/861–7660; 2020 Market St. at Church St.), sometimes calls to mind the scene in George Romero's *Dawn of the Dead* in which zombies invade the shopping mall. If you're looking for Pop-Tarts past midnight, you'll find a postapocalyptic scene of pierced and tattooed shoppers, many sporting that appealing new "smear" makeup look, and other creatures who only come out at night. But hey, they still have to eat. **CALA Foods** in the Castro (tel 415/431–3822; 4201 18th St. at Collingwood St.) is also open 24 hours. We'll spare you the neighborhood joke about the fresh fruits. Other all-night CALA locations include Haight and Stanyan, California and Hyde, and 6333 Geary.

The music of the night... When you need that certain CD, cassette, or even vinyl LP (remember those?) to create the soundtrack for your evening's escapades, several record stores are ready to accommodate you, and you'll find plenty of like-minded music addicts in the aisles till the last minute. Union Square's gigantic, three-story **Virgin Megastore** (tel 415/397–4525; 2 Stockton St. at Market St.; open Sun–Thurs till 11, Fri, Sat till midnight) features two floors of CDs and cassettes. It's a bit overwhelming—the video screens, the in-store disc jockey, the listening stations—but that's what makes it "mega." Skip the mediocre book department and cafe, but be sure to check out the CD import section, the best in the city. For a break, check out the stellar collection in the peaceful classical department. When you have to have that new Fugees CD at 11:59pm, the national **Tower Records** chain has two S.F. locations you can run to (tel 415/621–0588, 2280 Market St. at Noe St.; tel 415/885–0500; Columbus Ave. at Bay St.; both open daily 9am–midnight). The Castro location is heavy on dance and ambient music, appealing to the young club-hopping tripsters who frequent the neighborhood and work in the store; the opera section is also mind-boggling, a tribute to one of the city's passions. The Fisherman's Wharf location is larger and offers a much wider selection. The vocals section, in particular, can't be beat, and for classical fans, there's a separate annex across the street. Both Tower locations feature large newsstands and an OK selection of mostly pop culture–related books.

You need to know where the deejays shop? The tiny but well-stocked **CD Record Rack** (tel 415/552–4990; 3897 18th St. at Sanchez St.; open daily till 8 or later) gets all the latest imports and dance hits first, and staffers include hot deejays Phil B. of Pleasuredome and Jerry Bonham of V/SF, who can turn you on to the beat of the moment.

Vidiots... Yeah, we know, you're too busy night-crawling to bother with renting videos. But if you're a film geek, you'll get a contact high from the Inner Sunset's **Le Video** (tel 415/566–3606; 1239 9th Ave. at Irving St.; open daily till 11), a continual S.F. best-of-poll winner. It has an amazing selection of stuff you never knew existed on video, whole sections devoted to countries and auteur directors, a great Hong Kong action-flick selection, and a cult film section with hundreds of cheesy old soft-core porn flicks about big breasts. Weirdos—film-inclined or not—will thrill to the "cult" section, with its huge array of vintage sexploitation. **Leather Tongue Video** (tel 415/552–2900; 714 Valencia St. at 18th St.; open noon–11, until midnight Fri, Sat) is where the Mission's pierced, tattooed, and dyed-hair crowd turn for twisted, boundary-busting videos and amusing-to-appalling comix and zines. It has a terrifying supply of fun underground flicks to rent for parties. **Superstar Video** has two locations in the Castro, both open nightly until 11: The 17th Street location (tel 415/552–2253; 3989 17th St. at Market St.) specializes in classics, cult movies, and gay- and lesbian-themed films, with a small sampling of porn. The 18th Street location (tel 415/863–3333; 4141 18th St. near Castro) features a front room full of up-to-date first-run movies, and a second, inner room, crammed with primarily gay video, from the newest pretty-boy-factory releases to companies catering to the most infinitesimally specific tastes.

Toys and trinkets... Here are a few of our favorite open-late boutiques for fun, last-minute gifts or when you just want to feel like a kid again. **Quantity Postcards** in North Beach (tel 415/986–8866; 1441 Grant Ave.; Sun–Thurs till 11; Fri, Sat till 12:30) is crammed wall to wall and floor to ceiling with postcards—vintage postcards, futuristic postcards, funny postcards, shocking postcards, just-plain-weird postcards. And don't overlook the earthquake simulator, which for 50 cents gives you the dubious thrill of experiencing the Big One without the accompanying inconveniences. **Three Eighty One** (tel 415/621–3830; 381 Guerrero St. between 16th and 17th Sts.; open daily till 7, but they'll stay open later if you call ahead) is one-stop shopping for recovering Catholics and anyone who is thinking of starting a cult. This friendly but bizarre Mission district boutique is positively encrusted with eccentric gifts, most of them bordering on the sacrilegious, from the 3-D Shroud of Turin wallet cards to the Martyr Mousepads for your un-P.C. PC.

Uncle Mame's (tel 415/626–1953; 2193 Market St. at Sanchez St.; open daily till 9) knows well this simple truth: Toys are us, i.e., we are what we played with. This Castro shop provides a loving home for misfit toys and all-but-forgotten fads (check out the wall of Pez dispensers, from the Easter Bunny to Wonder Woman). Uncle Mame's is fun even when it's closed: people stand on the street and watch whole episodes of "Absolutely Fabulous," "The Sonny and Cher Show," and "Mary Hartman, Mary Hartman" on the cluster of vintage black-and-white TVs in the window. And it could only happen here (and even here, it could only happen in the Castro): A store/gallery/museum/shrine devoted exclusively to America's first voice, Barbra Streisand, called **Hello, Gorgeous!** (tel 415/864–2678; 549 Castro St.; open Tue–Thur till 7; Fri, Sat till 9; Sun till 6). The store features original works of devotional art from artists all over the country, collectibles and memorabilia, CDs, vinyl and videos, and even a Babs makeover station, where you can try on wigs representing her famous movie hairstyles and, of course, those lethal press-on nails like the ones Barbra brandished in *The Prince of Tides*. Jewish pastries and espresso are served. Like buttah!

Best views (for free)... Just about every inch of San Francisco offers a View. You can't get sick of the place or take it for granted—even old-timers still find themselves gasping once in a while. So don't be afraid to let your jaw slap your shoes when you behold our favorite 24-hour views, night sights, walk-ups and scenic drive-bys.

First, the overview: At 983 feet, the highest spot in San Francisco is **Mount Davidson** (reachable by Portola Dr.), crowned by a 103-foot concrete-and-steel cross. But you'll get an even more spectacular 360-degree view of the entire bay and the glittering city from atop the steep, windswept **Twin Peaks**, which overlook the Castro and Cole valleys and are reachable via Twin Peaks Boulevard. The early Spanish explorers called the twin hills "Los Pechos de la Chola," or "the breasts of the Indian girl," but prudish Americans must have thought that was too much of a mouthful. **Buena Vista Park**, a forested mountain at the beginning of Haight-Ashbury (Haight St. between Buena Vista Ave. East and Buena Vista Ave. West) offers great views of the Coast Range Mountains, from Mount Tamalpais to Mount Diablo, and the sparkling city lies at your feet. (A caution: BV Park is populated all night, as it's a preferred spot for the midnight rambles of some gay men. So be prepared to observe some wildlife.) For arguably the best view of the entire Bay Area, head up to the inarguably phallic **Coit Tower**. But don't drive—you'll be stuck waiting in your car. Walk up from North Beach or Telegraph Hill, or up the **Filbert Steps** off Sansome Street, leaving the noisy city for the lush, fragrant gardens that hug the winding, wooden steps to the tower. Too tired to climb? A drive up (and up and up) California Street to the majestic **Fairmont Hotel** (tel 415/772–5000; 950 Mason St. at California St.) is enough to induce vertigo, but it doesn't match the Cinemascope citywide vision offered by the posh hotel's outdoor glass elevator. Look at the pretty lights *waaaaaay* down below and try hard not to think about Jennifer Jones falling to her death in *The Towering Inferno*. Then, look back on all the places you've been from the **Golden Gate Bridge**, which offers a diorama-like view of the sparkling city, the bay below, and is pretty damn postcard-perfect itself. You can drive, walk, or even ride a bike across it, though we don't recommend cycling it at night).

Best views (for a fee)... Yeah, it's touristy, but there's a reason that tourists flock to the **Cliff House** (tel 415/386–3330; 1090 Point Lobos Ave.). It has several dining

SAN FRANCISCO (HANGING OUT

settings, from a kooky saloon to a fine linen-tablecloth room. Do whatever you must to get a sundown window seat. The **Equinox Room** at the Hyatt Regency Hotel (tel 415/ 788–1234; 2 Market St., top floor) is the city's only revolving restaurant (one is enough, don't you think?), and even though the more recent high-rise buildings get in the way a bit, it's still a grand view. (Voyeurs look forward to when the restaurant spins their table back in line with the towering apartment complex across the street). Vertigo lovers will also enjoy looking down on the ride up in the glass elevator.

Harry Denton's Starlight Room, in the Sir Francis Drake Hotel (tel 415/395–8595; 450 Powell St.) not only boasts a knockout view, but gives high rollers a glimpse back at another era, of cigar-smoking high times and obviously mercenary blonds on the arms of obviously older gentlemen. It sure ain't the food (or the prices, or the service, or the convenience of location, or parking) that keeps bringing visitors back to **Julius' Castle** (tel 415/362–3042; 1541 Montgomery St.). It's the sweeping views, north and east over the bay, that take in the maritime movements and the sparkling lights. This restaurant in a former mansion on Telegraph Hill is one of the most romantic places in town.

If money is no object, give us a call, and we'll ride a cable car with you to the Mark Hopkins Hotel, then rocket in the elevator up to the 19th-floor sky-room bar called **Top of the Mark** (tel 415/392–3434; California and Mason Sts.). We'll sport for the cable car fare if you get the drinks; the panoramic views are priceless. The other most expensive view you can get in the city, short of buying a house on Nob Hill, is from the jackets-required **Carnelian Room**, a 52nd-floor bar/lounge atop the Bank of America building (tel 415/433–7500; 555 California St.) in the heart of San Francisco's "Wall Street West." The real San Francisco treat is a ride on one of the city's world-famous **cable cars**. For just $2 for a nontransferable one-way ticket (buy it from the conductor as you board) you get the most enjoyable ride in town, with great views and people-watching as well as breathtaking roller-coaster thrills. Out of the original 30 that served the city, there are three surviving lines (restored in 1984 to the tune of some $60 million): the Powell-Mason, the Powell-Hyde, and the California. They run up and down hills at 9.5 miles per hour until 12:30am, and that's when they're the most fun—with the tourists all snug in their hotels, they're almost empty. Ride on the outside, hold on tight, feel the breeze, and take in those distinctively S.F. sights, sounds, and smells.

Best walks… San Francisco is a walker's city. It's better to leave your car in the hotel parking lot than risk the frustration and probable tickets in this town that's long on charm and notoriously short on legal parking spaces.

S.F. has some 350 stairways, most of them in residential areas, and the neighbors often voluntarily beautify them with amazing gardens. They've even inspired a book of their own (*Stairway Walks in San Francisco*, by Adah Bakalinsky; Wilderness Press, 2440 Bancroft Way, Berkeley, CA 94704; tel 510/843–8080). A few favorites: the wooden **Filbert Steps**, mentioned above, which rise up a steep sheer cliff from Sansome Street to Montgomery Street beneath **Coit Tower**, affording grand views of the Bay Area, the city—and plenty of primo make-out spots to boot. Above the Castro, in the neighborhood known as Lower Terrace, you'll find the **Saturn Stairs**. Like the Filbert Steps, they're surrounded by the lush gardening contributions of the neighbors. Besides, the houses are charming, and the streets have names like Jupiter, Mars, and yep, Uranus. After you've caught your breath from the steep climb up Nob Hill to the magnificent **Grace Cathedral**, walk the outdoor labyrinth, which is set in colored concrete in front of the Cathedral. It's a replica of the ancient meditative, spiritual path in the Cathedral at Chartres, and if you do it right, it takes about 20 minutes to go in and back out again, and you're guaranteed to gain an insight or two while losing some more calories.

If you'd rather walk on the water, it's easily done in San Francisco. **Ocean Beach**, at end of Golden Gate Park, is a 3-mile strip along the Pacific, perfect for windswept walks, sunset to sunrise, solo or with a romantic partner. On the walk along **Golden Gate Promenade**, a 3.5-mile stretch from Aquatic Park down to the Golden Gate Bridge and Fort Point, you'll pass yachts, the Palace of Fine Arts, ritzy Marina homes, and spectacular views of the bridge and the mystical Marin Headlands. And now, out to the water. Spotlit until late in the night, the **Palace of Fine Arts** (3601 Lyon St. between Jefferson and Bay

Sts.) is an incredibly romantic walking spot near the Marina. Built in 1915 for the post-earthquake Panama Pacific Exposition, the palace is a ready-made ruins, a classical Roman rotunda in the midst of a small park with swans swimming on a sweet, artificial lake. Fisherman's Wharf is generally anathema to locals unless they have out-of-town visitors, but the tourist mecca called **Pier 39**, at the end of Stockton Street, has its own special charm after the tourists have gone back to their hotels. When the fog horns are honking, the sea lions are barking, and cable cars come clanging, it's like being in a romantic late-night-movie version of San Francisco.

While you're in the vicinity of Fisherman's Wharf, take a stroll through the **100 Quince Trees** that late sculptor Art Grant planted in the shape of a block-sized heart on Bay Street between Hyde and Leavenworth: Could this be the heart that Tony Bennett left in San Francisco?

Readings and gallery openings... Readings are one of the best entertainment values in the city—they're free. And you can hear some great writing when you're not wincing into your espresso over a particularly embarrassing stretch of confessional poetry. And like a good hockey game, a poetry slam can always turn into a poetry brawl. Check out the spoken-word listings in the free weekly papers and *Poetry Flash*, a free monthly poetry tabloid (imagine that!). There are readings regularly at **Paradise Lounge** (tel 415/861–6906; 1501 Folsom St.; Sun at 8); **Chameleon** (tel 415/821–1891; 853 Valencia St.; Mon at 9); **Jammin' Java** (tel 415/668–5282; Cole St. at Waller St.; Wednesdays at 8) and **Café International** (tel 415/552–7390; 508 Haight St. at Fillmore St.; Fri at 8).

Gallery openings are another entertainment bargain—a good source of free food and drink and sometimes even an artistic epiphany. The first Thursday of the month is traditionally the night for art-show receptions; look for fliers in coffee shops and scan the local papers for announcements. Check out the alternative galleries **Southern Exposure** (tel 415/863–2141; 401 Alabama St.), **Architrave** (tel 415/621–4923; 541 Hayes St.), which feels like a museum of the future and displays fine art and furniture, and **New Langton Arts** (tel 415/ 626–5416; 1246 Folsom St.), an often-controversial arts space in a second-floor South of Market loft. And make sure to make a pilgrimage to **Keane Eyes Gallery** (tel 415/ 922–9309; 651 Market St. at 6th St.), home of San Francisco's most famous painter, Margaret Keane, who is still turning out those huge-eyed kids and puppies, without a hint of irony.

Museums in the dark... On Thursdays, the new **San Francisco Museum of Modern Art** (tel 415/357–4000; 151 3rd St.) keeps the galleries open until 9pm, and admission is half-price. You can browse the museum store until 9:30 or dine at Caffé Museo till 9. On the third Thursday of every month, there's also live jazz in the galleries.

At the **Guinness Museum of World Records** (tel 415/771–9890; 235 Jefferson St. near Fisherman's Wharf), you can view a famous collection of weirdness: the biggest, smallest, fattest, fastest, etc., until 11 every night. The nearby **Medieval Dungeon** (tel 415/885–4834; 107 Jefferson St.; open daily till 11:30) is a torture museum, boasting "more than 40 barbaric exhibits of torture and annihilation." Inside this gorefest in wax, you'll hear Gregorian chants punctuated by hideous (prerecorded) shrieks.

late nigh

t dining

New Yorkers eat out
because they live in small
boxes with toaster ovens
instead of kitchens.
Consequently, every New
Yorker is a restaurant
expert, with a specialization

"Kindred: The Embraced" featured rival vampire clans competing for dominion over the city's O-positive citizens like warring Mafia families.

Now, we all know that vampires get hungry after dark. But they have a specialized taste and know just where to go to get what they want. What about the rest of us nightcrawlers? Where do we turn to satisfy more conventional appetites when the moon is high?

Well, when the day lights die down and the night lights come up sparkling, the visual takes a back seat to the other senses—especially smell and taste. Breathe in the aromas of San Francisco: the roasting coffee in North Beach and countless neighborhood cafes, the sourdough and seafood of Fisherman's Wharf, the Asian/Mexican/Italian spices of Chinatown and the Mission, the wood-burning grills of Pacific Heights....

With one restaurant for every 230 people, San Francisco spends more per capita on eating out than any other city in the U.S. It's one of the most ethnically, culturally diverse cities in the country, too, and you can taste it in the menus. People talk about restaurants here the way they talk about sports teams in less food-blessed cities, and follow trades and achievements of star chefs as if they were multimillion-dollar pitchers or quarterbacks.

But let's tell the truth here: San Francisco suffers from a drought as far as good late-night dining goes—"the tyranny of the Daytime People," as one of our nocturnal friends puts it. With a few exceptions, most of the really great restaurants close at 10, 11 at the outside. The simple truth is San Franciscans tend to eat early—the dinner rush happens between 7 and 8, which means you can saunter into **Stars** or **Postrio** after 9 and sit right down.

This is one of the few downsides of the city—it fancies itself a cosmopolitan player on a par with New York and L.A., but it goes to bed early. The loss in 1995 of the Brasserie in the basement of the Fairmont Hotel left a huge gap: This was a place you could go dressed up at 4am and still feel like you were out on the town. Sure, there are lots of places where you can get junk food at all hours in trashy and fun atmospheres, but there's not much as far as glamorous dining goes.

As for those that do stay open late, be forewarned that this is California, and even the restaurants can be kind of whimsical about their hours—they'll close earlier than scheduled if business is slow or the weather is bad or they're just not into it, man. The good side of the California thing is you can pretty much wear whatever you want (except where otherwise noted).

The Lowdown

Après-club... Wandering and wondering where to go after the clubs have closed and you're totally munched out? All-nighters are sure to find dim lighting and sympathetic fellow insomniacs at these nocturnal haunts. In the South of Market nightclub ghetto, **Pizza Love** is the closest thing when you bounce out the door, but its proximity is about all it has going for it. Still, it's open late, and you'll find plenty of company to compare post-club notes with. Half of the historic, beloved Polk Gulch greasy spoon called **Grubstake** (open daily until 4am) is an original railroad car that served the transportation line between Berkeley, Oakland, and San Francisco at the turn of the century. The other half is a new kitchen and dining room. You can get cooked-to-order burgers and breakfasts, but the real steal is their Portuguese dinner every Saturday night.

"Doobie doobie doo...." That's Frank Sinatra crooning "Strangers in the Night" on the jukebox at your window booth at **It's Tops**, a hole-in-the wall, knotty-pine-paneled, family-run Market Street diner serving breakfast till the wee hours since 1935. The waitpeople are all characters, of course (Tasha is a dead ringer for Sydney on "Melrose Place," and she thinks nothing of joining in on your most intimate conversation). Down Market Street in the Castro, the greasy spoon called **Orphan Andy's** is beloved because it's always there, always welcoming, even at the darkest, bleakest, hungriest hour of the night. The look is vintage diner, the lighting has a helpful and forgiving reddish glow, you can get breakfast or burgers at any hour, and the help is sassy and fun. Nearby, the 24-hour lesbian-run diner **Bagdad Cafe** is more of a scene. Again, the food is dependable, not outstanding, but there's a surprisingly broad range, from late-night life-savers like good pancakes and waffles with fresh fruit, to specials like well-seasoned risotto and grilled seafood (but the desserts look

better than they taste). Bagdad is a bit too brightly lit—
for the post-club photosensitive sort, it can be like eating
in a supermarket. But use the high wattage to check out
the waiters' funny name tags. Working a fake-fifties-cum-
early-eighties look, with neon-lit black-and-white tile
and glass brick, **Sparky's** is overpriced but has better food
than its two Castro siblings (the pizzas and malteds are
good bets, and you can get omelettes if you're into it).

Some people swear the Castro's **Hot N' Hunky** is
the best burger in town, but that may be mostly because
there's not an awful lot of competition after midnight. In
the Marina, **Mel's Drive In** is a neato, spic-and-span
diner straight out of *American Graffiti*, where you can
order up the standard diner fare or low-fat, healthy stuff
like veggieburgers. And you can play "I Left My Heart in
San Francisco" on your tabletop jukebox and no one will
think you're corny.

Nosh around the clock... A moment of silence, please,
for the late, lamented Brasserie, which for decades
embraced San Francisco's tired and hungry 24 hours a
day in the basement of the Fairmont Hotel, and gave
staying out late an elegant ending point.... Thank you.
The town's remaining all-nighters are less gracious, but
we're grateful for them just the same. We've already mentioned the coffee and all-night-breakfasts at **Bagdad
Cafe** and **Orphan Andy's** in the Castro, and the nearby
Sparky's, all of them dependable, never-say-close haunts
where you'll no doubt spot people you flirted with or
frosted in the club just an hour ago. Downtown, on
Mason Street, there's a strip of all-night cafes near the
legit theaters on Geary and just far enough from the
other sort of theaters that are popular in the Tenderloin.
Among them, **Cafe Mason** and **Lori's Diner** are
dependable and serve decent grub, and are, of course,
chock-full of happy, hungry drunks after last call. On
Fridays and Saturdays only, **Mel's Drive In** in the Marina
stays open and rocks 'round the clock with an attractive
crowd of ravenous straight singles. And when the best
surprise is no surprise, you can always opt for those bea-
cons of the pan-American post-midnight munchies, the
surpassingly ugly, seafoam-green, airport-sized **Denny's**
in Japantown and the indistinguishable-from-the-rest
International House of Pancakes in the Marina.

Your basic burgers and dogs... Something about the night brings out the beast inside us, makes us crave the all-American grub we'd be embarrassed to order by the light of day. But this being San Francisco, the basics often come with an odd twist. Eighty-year-old *Chronicle* columnist Herb Caen, "Mr. San Francisco" himself, swears the hot dog at 32-year-old **Clown Alley** is the best in the city. With its circus-colored, clown-shaped sign, this family-run burger stand/diner with indoor and outdoor seating has long been a friendly beacon on many an inebriated North Beach night. Caen doesn't get to the Mission too much, though—if he did, we'd sport him to a red vinyl booth at our favorite dog-and-burger show, **Burger Joint**, a friendly, unpretentious place with an extremely limited menu (burgers, hot dogs, fries, sodas, and thick shakes), and a spacious, space-age atmosphere that somehow manages to be both retro and futuristic at once. The burgers are made with trendy Niman-Schell organic beef, the chicken breast sandwiches are made with free-range chicken, natch, and you can get a decent veggieburger here, too. Good old **Hamburger Mary's** lost a lot of its attic-like charm when the owners remodeled and cleaned up the clutter, but the SOMA/Mission institution is still the place to eat fabulous burgers with fabulous people. This is where the straight, 11th Street clubgoers mingle with the Folsom Street gay leather crowd. Carnivores congregate at **Tommy's Joynt**, a big beerhall of a place with a huge mural on the outside of the building and a rowdy, old-style saloon atmosphere inside, complete with beef-carving stations and popcorn and peanut "vendors"—actually, it's not unlike eating at a stadium.

See-and-be-scenes... Where to go to see stars? Or to be seen? You have to keep up with your *People* magazine and E! network–watching: There's no dress code in San Francisco (what's a maitre d' to do?) and that shlump in torn jeans and T-shirt might really be a movie mogul or Microsoft multimillionaire, while that drop-dead dressed-to-the-nines gorgeous couple could be a penniless pair of retro-infatuated club kids with good bone structure and a knack for thrift shopping. Sometimes you can tell just by the name: Take **Stars**, for example. Ten years after it splashed and sparkled its way onto the S.F. scene, Jeremiah Tower's famous, always-buzzing bistro has mediocre food and is way too crowded and noisy, but everyone still goes, hoping to make the scene. Primo tables: "The Club," right under the wall of celebrity photos (good luck!). Despite the kitchen's disappointments, the desserts are still among the best in town—the signature star-shaped, chocolate-centered cookie is a take-home treasure. Just around the corner is Stars' streamlined sister, **Stars Cafe**, good when you need a quick bite before or after the opera or ballet.

Next stop on our star tour: **Rubicon**, the fine Union Square restaurant owned by Francis Ford Coppola, Robert De Niro, and Robin Williams, all of whom can actually be seen there now and then, eating the French-inspired combinations conjured by up-and-coming star chef Traci des Jardins. There's a nightly three-course prix fixe menu and master sommelier Larry Stone's wondrous wine list. At **Postrio**, northern outpost of L.A. celebrichef Wolfgang Puck, you can get a Californian/Mediterranean menu—and Puck's famously thin, crisp California pizzas. You'll also get a snootful of S.F. society—it's like stepping straight into Pat Steger's hugely amusing weekly society column in the *Chronicle*. It's not for the faint of heart or socially insecure—there's a hideous stairway down the very center of the restaurant; when you walk down, everyone turns and stares. **Moose's** is a new North Beach institution for nouvelle Italian created by Ed and Mary Etta Moose, who created an old North Beach institution, the **Washington Square Bar & Grill** (nicknamed the "Washbag"). Located just across the square from each other, both are good places to look for journalists and newsmakers. While Moose's is a big, airy room, Washington is an older, smaller, crabbier, clubby place. Fans of "Nash Bridges," the new Don Johnson TV series set in S.F., will recognize **Bix**, a twenties-style downtown deco dining oasis in the shadow of the Transamerica Pyramid, a place where a woman can wear a cocktail hat while picking at a Waldorf salad with roquefort or Russian osetra caviar with crème fraîche and toast points. **Miss Pearl's Jam House** is a soul-kitchen magnet for touring rock stars, who tend to favor the neighboring Phoenix Hotel and then raid chef Wesley Saunders' refrigerators for dependably good Jamaican food, like mountains of cumin rice and black beans topped with jerk chicken, Caribbean red fries, or peppery Rasta pasta.

When in Cali... Let them argue over who created California cuisine—was it Jeremiah Tower or Alice Waters? Begun in the seventies, it continues to explore and develop in the nineties, and we love its seemingly common-sense traits: an emphasis on fresh, local, often organic produce, cross-cultural influences, grilling, sautéing, salads, and aesthetically beautiful presentation. One of the city's most popular California cuisine eatspots, the sleek, stylish **Fog City Diner** almost single-handedly began the diner trend when it opened its chrome-and-glass doors near Levi-Strauss Plaza a decade ago, and it still wears the crown. Sure you can get a burger and fries—but the ketchup will be homemade and the burger arrives on toasted foccacia bread. You can order imitation Rice-A-Roni here—and we actually recommend it! It's made from scratch in the kitchen, and it's unbelievably tender and spicy, the way the San Francisco Treat should be. When money's no object, or you just need to make yourself feel posh, turn to the sleek, glass-fronted yupscale **Zuni Cafe**, a Hayes Valley perennial that keeps its doors open until midnight most nights. After a margarita or a glass of wine at the long copper bar, hope for a spot in the main dining room, and then hope your friends and rivals can see you ostentatiously enjoying oysters and the best Caesar in town.

Neighborhood favorites... San Francisco's personality is in its distinct neighborhoods, and each neighborhood has at least one special restaurant to be proud of. Seafood is the password at **Aqua**: The downtown eatery's facade is unmarked, but a fish-tail door handle marks the spot. Inside, you'll find swimming-pool colors and enormous floral arrangements, and the freshest, most exquisitely prepared seafood in the city. You *will* wait for a table at the Haight's kitschy-cool **Cha Cha Cha**—the wait can get up to two hours for a seat in this tiny, color-saturated hotspot where you can consume spicy tapas and Cuban/Cajun combos like fried calamari, plantains, black beans and rice, and big pitchers of fruity sangria. And locals do wait, happily. Besides, the wait gives you time to take a stroll through the Haight and soak in the sights and sounds of the vintage- and head-shop-choked neighborhood. South of Market, the cool, artsy crowd heads for the **Slow Club**, a pleasingly dim, unhurried deco/industrial cafe where the diners graze on Niman-Schell organic beef burgers, incredible fries (with just a dusting of herbs), and good mix-and-match Mediterranean-style tapas-sized items. Amid the multiculti competition of the Mission district, you can't do much better than **Ti Couz**, an affordable, crowded, and friendly crêperie where the paper-thin Breton-style buckwheat pancakes enfold all sorts of surprises: ratatouille, cheeses, almond butter—and our favorite, Nutella and bananas with a scoop of homemade vanilla ice cream.

The lively Castro district, which is otherwise filled with diners, cafes, and ethnic eateries, finally has the fine dining establishment it deserves: John Cunin, creator of the visually exuberant Cypress Club (see "Only in S.F." below), has done it with **2223 Market**. His sort-of no-name restaurant is low-key, even austere, and the emphasis is on the elegantly down-home food, like the wild-mushroom pasta and roasted monkfish. Order anything if it comes with the garlic mashed potatoes.

Stars of the Orient... Chinatown is as famous an attraction as almost anything else in the city, and it's a fascinating, eerie, and atmospheric place for a nighttime walk. You'll feel far, far away from America (as if you didn't already feel that way merely being in San Francisco!). Strangely, restaurants in Chinatown don't stay open till the wee hours as they do in some other cities. Still, you can find choice Chinese in various locations around town. Open until 3am on weekends, **Great Eastern** is the exception to Chinatown's early closings. You'll want to write a postcard about the authentic Cantonese food—and maybe some of the film people you spot here—but the fluorescent bathroom-light atmosphere takes some getting used to. If you're not scared by things like octopus, pork feet with jellyfish, and sliced steelhead, order what the Chinese family at a nearby table is having. Otherwise stick to familiar things like the kung pao chicken. Popular with a young, non-Chinese crowd, **Brandy Ho's** is the new side of Chinatown; in fact it looks more like a brand-new brass-and-marble Italian eatery than any Chinese restaurant we've ever seen. But the fiery, Hunan-style food is among the best in the area and worth a visit if you can beat the midnight weekend closing. Culinary innovation is evident at **Flying Kamikaze's Rock & Roll Sushi**, in the straight singles' playground called the Marina district.

The name almost screams: "We're fun, noisy, and irreverent." And it is. Think sake slushes, ahi tuna dumplings, combo rolls, and a raucous soundtrack for sushi-eating.

A little Italy... Yeah, San Francisco is known for Chinese food, but its Italian food is justly famous, too: Head for the bustling, tourist-dense micro-Italy called North Beach and take a late-night stroll: You'll find dozens of little family-run Italian spots, many of which will stay open as long as there are customers. Old-time North Beachers and tourists meet at the city's first and still favorite sidewalk cafe, **Enrico's**, where you can sit on the heated sidewalk patio consuming pizzas, pastas, and now tapas, and watch the remains of the North Beach scene (Look: There goes a punk, a hippie, a beatnik!). If you don't mind garlic breath, we can heartily recommend the touristy but good **The Stinking Rose**, an all-garlic restaurant. And we mean ALL garlic. There's even a garlic ice cream. Non-garlic items are marked on the menu with a little vampire icon. **LuLu**, a laid-back, noisy, fun Calitalian hotspot near the Moscone Convention Center, has a soaring, skylit ceiling, massive wood-burning oven, memorable Mediterranean menu, and brightly colored plates that are sometimes too big for the tables. At **Vivande**, near the opera house, you'll find rustic, lusty, homemade pastas, lots of Italian wines on the lengthy list, and a large, ornate room with an umber-and-amber glow, like a dream of Tuscany. If you're simply in a hurry, find one of the three pleasingly spartan **Pasta Pomodoro** locations for good, fast, cheap spaghetti, cappellini, penne, linguini—what have you—plus salads and Italian sandwiches served at the counter or to go.

Latin (b)eats... If there's any one thing that unites San Franciscans across all class, economic, racial, age, sexual, and other boundaries, it's the humble burrito. Big, cheap, and relatively good for you, custom-built by assembly line, served up in a casual, cheerful cantina atmosphere, burritos have become a staple food of San Franciscans. If you want the real thing, go to the Mission. You'll have to stand in what is often a long line for your burrito at **Taqueria Pancho Villa**, a big, friendly, family-style cafeteria in the Mission. But the line moves fast and the carne asada burrito or the super-veggie (on your choice of a plain, red tomato, or green spinach tortilla) are well worth the wait.

There's also an abundance of ways to have your burrito done up at the stripped-down **Taqueria Zapata** in the Castro, which offers great cruising from its glassed-in corner spot, if you're up for it. **Bad Man Jose's**, a snug burrito parlor in the heart of the Castro, serves up healthy, delicious California burritos and garden-veggie tacos in a setting that looks both ancient and high-tech Mexican. Check out the tasty *tiburon* (shark meat) burrito and bite back. For a fancier sit-down situation, head for the Mission's colorful **La Rondalla**, where the festive Christmas lights stay up year-round, and you can eat your after-midnight huevos rancheros to the inimitably cheerful sound of live mariachi music.

Hello deli... "This is a good place for a diet," says the sign on the outside of the door at **Max's Opera Cafe**, kittycorner from the new Museum of Modern Art and Moscone Center. "This is a bad place for a diet," says the other side of the door. Too late. You can get everything in huge proportions at this Manhattan/Miami-style deli, including mile-high sandwiches and desserts. The Opera Plaza location of this institution has a gimmick—operatic singing waiters—which may be a reason to skip it. **David's Delicatessen** on Geary, right across from the renovated Curran Theatre, has been around forever. But what it lacks in looks, this deli makes up in flavor—David's serves up authentic New York–style, half-pound sammitches (pastrami, Reuben) and more than 100 desserts, including cheesecake, of course, and five-chocolate Decadence. Great before or after a show.

Only in S.F.... There are a lot of wonderfully exotic, only-in-S.F. dining experiences around, and some, luckily, can be experienced late at night. A survivor of the 1906 Big One, **Eichelberger's** has turned into a cultural mecca—though Jesse Helms might find it nightmarish. Named after the late legendary drag artist Ethel Eichelberger, this Mission/Potrero Hill nightspot serves up cabaret drag acts (banjo players, cross-gendered singers on trapezes) with funky bar snacks and seasonal California cuisine (yummy Caesar salads and grilled duck with pears) in Egyptian-inspired surroundings. At **Kan Zaman** in the Haight, you're encouraged to get comfy and crosslegged on purple velvet floor pillows, grooving to Middle Eastern music while sampling tasty Mediterranean foods like hummus, dolmas, and spanokopita. You can even take a hit of apricot-flavored tobacco from an enormous hookah straight out of *Alice in Wonderland*. The Fat Chance Belly Dancers undulate on weekend nights, and nobody will mind at all if you decide you have to get up and wiggle your hips. The Multimedia Gulch crowd plugs into the good, basic bar vittles at **Icon Byte**, a weird, wired restaurant, nightclub, and Internet-connected South of Market cybercafe. **Take Orders** is a self-described "uniform restaurant" in the Mission with a serious military fixation. The whole place is painted in camouflage patterns, the interior is set up like a mess hall (if mess halls had bars), and if you wear a uniform you get a discount on the basic diner fare—burgers, sandwiches, salads, breakfast anytime.

A slice is a slice... In any city, you can be sure to start an argument by declaring your allegiance to a certain pizza. Pizza is like a Rorschach test: Some like it thin and crispy, some like it thick and chewy, some don't like tomato sauce (can you imagine?). Post-clubbing, there's **Pizza Love**, in the SOMA nightclub ghetto, sitting right next to DNA and Slim's (see The Club Scene). The pizza is Easy-Bake Oven bad, and the crowd is late-night zombies, but it's convenient, and drunk people aren't picky. **Escape From New York** has good, New York–style, thin-crust pizza at three locations. While you wait for a slice at the Castro location, look at the celebrity-photo wall, which features signed pix of John Waters, Shelly Winters, and other pizzaphiles. For that famous, fancy, California pizza, go for **Vicolo** near the opera house and Symphony Hall, where you take your pick of gourmet toppings on a cornmeal pie crust. A more radical form of California-ization of pizza can be found at **Extreme Pizza** in Pacific Heights, where you can get humongous baked-to-order slices and eat them at a picnic table made of snowboards. If you can't decide between nachos, pizza, or salad, come here, and you can have all three on one spicy slab. The friendly place is staffed by college jocks and skate dudes, and if you want a whole pizza you have to take it home and bake it yourself. Our favorite, though, is **North Beach Pizza**. Not only is it arguably (we warned you) the best in the city (we love the pesto Verdi pizza), but it also delivers 24–7.

Sugar rush... Isn't it strange how that sweet tooth gets its most intense cravings after dark? Luckily, San Francisco has several distinctive ice-cream parlors where you can be sure of getting your just desserts until about 11 every night. **Polly Ann Ice Cream** is an exotic (okay, weird) ice-cream parlor in the Sunset district that serves up 50 unheard-of flavors each day (from among 400), including Bumpy Road and durian, a vaguely gasoline-scented scoop made from the equally rank tropical fruit. If you just can't decide, owner Charles Wu will let you spin the roulette wheel of flavors. You'll want to get a double-dip of the homemade ice creams at **Mitchell's Ice Cream**, a more old-fashioned, family-run San Francisco ice-cream parlor in the Mission, because the Hawaiian and Portuguese flavors (avocado, baby coconut, Mexican chocolate, orchid) are so unique. It's sort of like getting your ice cream at the bank, though, because they hand you your cone from behind bulletproof Plexiglas (okay—that part isn't so old-fashioned). The unbelievably rich and fattening scoops at the homegrown **Double Rainbow** chain have been named best in the country on more than one occasion. You can get your Ultra-Chocolate triple-dip at DR locations in the Castro, Polk Gulch, and West Portal.

Need a cop?... Like any other place that deserves to call itself a city, San Francisco features a plethora of 24-hour doughnut shops. Drag queens take note: Set your make-up mirror on "day" setting; for some reason, doughnut shops (and supermarkets) favor fluorescent lighting. If you get a sugar craving while clubbing South of Market, you can head for **All Star Donuts** (399 5th at Harrison), near the End Up, or **Happy Donuts** (761 3rd at King), which is close to 177 Townsend (home of Pleasuredome and Universe) and the King Street Garage (home of Futura). Downtown, there's **Bell's Donuts** (6 6th between Market and Mission), **Bob's Donuts & Pastry Shop** (1621 Polk between Sacramento and Clay), near all the Polk Street gay bars, and **Van Ness Bakery & Cafe** (1122 Van Ness between Geary and Post). In the Castro, there's **Rolling Pin Donuts** (497 Castro between Market and 18th), which also sometimes has pizza, and **Magic Donuts** (2400 Mission at 24th). These, in our opinion, are the crème de la crème–filled handful of 24-hour S.F. doughnut joints.

The Index

Aqua. Seafood with splashy style, as famous for its towers of fresh flowers as it is for chef Michael Mina's wondrous way with fresh fish.... *Tel 415/956–9662. 252 California St. between Front and Battery Sts.; Embarcadero BART/MUNI Metro stop; California cable car; F streetcar; 1, 42 MUNI bus. Reservations recommended. Jacket and tie recommended. Open until 11.*

Bad Man Jose's. Huge, fresh, health-conscious burritos and other Mexican fast food—whole-wheat tortillas, black beans, brown rice—in a cozy, relaxed setting.... *Tel 415/861–1706. 4077 18th St. between Noe and Castro Sts.; Castro BART/MUNI Metro stop; F streetcar; 24, 33 MUNI bus. Open until 11. No credit cards.*

Bagdad Cafe. 'Round-the-clock Eggs with Attitude at this dependable Castro post-club catch-all, which is sometimes so brightly lit you gotta wear sunglasses at night.... *Tel 415/621–4434. 2295 Market St. at 16th St.; Castro BART/MUNI Metro stop, F streetcar, 37 MUNI bus. No credit cards.*

Bix. You can have a complete meal, complete with tablecloth, right at the gorgeous bar in this sexy, mysterious art deco speakeasy, featuring smoky, saxy jazz, one of the town's best martinis, and really good champagnes by the glass.... *Tel 415/433–6300. 56 Gold St. between Sutter and Montgomery Sts.; Montgomery BART/MUNI Metro stop; 12, 42 MUNI bus. Reservations recommended. Open Sunday until 10:30, Mon–Thur until 11, Fri–Sat until midnight.*

Brandy Ho's. Looks like an Italian restaurant at first, but the fiery Hunan cooking makes you see everything differently—after your eyes stop watering. Popular with a young, late-night non-Chinese crowd.... *Tel 415/788–7527. 217 Columbus*

Ave. between Pacific Ave. and Broadway; 15, 41, 83 MUNI bus. Open until 11, Fri–Sat until midnight.

Burger Joint. Sort of a retro-futuristic White Castle, with great grilled burgers, hot dogs, sublime fries, and milkshakes. The kind of place that looks better at night.... Tel 415/824–3494. 807 Valencia St. at 19th St.; 26, 33 MUNI bus. Open until 11. No credit cards.

Cafe Mason. The weird decor in this cheery 24-hour diner includes fountains that rain sporadically from what look like fluorescent light fixtures into what look like giant aquariums in the middle of the restaurant. We had to ask—the waitress says they keep the restaurant humid for all the orchids.... Tel 415/544–0320. 320 Mason St. between Geary and O'Farrell Sts.; Powell BART/MUNI Metro stop, F streetcar, 38 MUNI bus. Open 24 hours.

Cha Cha Cha. Can you say "sharing"? Everyone will want to sample a bunch of spicy tapas-sized items at this intensely colorful (and popular) Haight hotspot.... Tel 415/386–5758. 1801 Haight St. at Shrader St.; 6, 7, 43 MUNI bus. Open until 11, Fri–Sat until 11:30.

Clown Alley. Herb Caen, Mr. San Francisco himself, says this North Beach mom-and-pop burger stand has the best hot dog in San Francisco.... Tel 415/421–2540. 42 Columbus Ave. at Jackson St.; 15, 41 MUNI bus. Open until 11, Fri until 3, Sat until 2:30. No credit cards.

David's Delicatessen. Somewhat sad-looking deli that serves up authentic New York–style half-pound sandwiches (pastrami, Reuben), and more than 100 desserts.... Tel 415/771–1600. 474 Geary St. between Mason and Taylor Sts.; Powell BART/MUNI Metro stop, F streetcar, 38 MUNI bus. Open until midnight.

Denny's. After all-night bowling at Japantown Bowl next door, you can order "Moons Over My Hammy" at this amphitheater-sized 24-hour last resort, decorated in hideous seafoam pastels.... Tel 415/563–1400. 1700 Post St. between Webster and Laguna Sts., 38 MUNI bus. Open 24 hours.

Double Rainbow. Best ice cream in the city, if not the country.... Tel 415/621–2350, 407 Castro St. at Market St. (in the Castro); Castro BART/MUNI Metro stop, F streetcar, 24 MUNI bus. Tel 415/821–3420, 3939 24th St. between Sanchez and Noe Sts. (In Noe Valley); 24, 48 MUNI bus. Tel 415/668–6690, 1724 Haight St. between Cole and Shrader Sts. (in the Haight); 43, 66 MUNI bus. Open until 11.

Eichelberger's. This former flophouse survived the Big One of 1906; now it's where Dan Quayle's dreaded cultural elite (drag queens, performance artists) meet to eat.... Tel 415/863–4177. 2742 17th St. at Florida St.; 12, 22, 33 MUNI bus. Open Fri and Sat until 1.

Enrico's. The city's first and still favorite sidewalk cafe, where you can sit on the heated sidewalk patio and devour pizza, pasta, and tapas. A North Beach institution.... Tel 415/982–6223. 504 Broadway at Kearny St.; 15, 41, 83 MUNI bus. Reservations recommended. Open until 11, Fri–Sat until midnight.

Escape From New York Pizza. Authentic New York thin-crust pizza with nods to California taste (artichokes, broccoli, sun-dried tomatoes).... Tel 415/252–1515, 508 Castro St. between 18th and 19th Sts. (in the Castro); Castro BART/MUNI Metro stop; F streetcar; 24, 33 MUNI bus. Tel 415/668–5577, 1737 Haight St. between Cole and Shrader Sts. (in the Haight); 43, 66 MUNI bus. Open Mon–Wed until 1, Thur–Sat until 2, Sun until midnight.

Extreme Pizza. Giant slabs of new wave pizza made to order, with fresh salads and microbrews served up by cheerful Hootie & The Blowfish fans.... Tel 415/929–9900. 1730 Fillmore St. between Post and Sutter Sts.; 2, 3, 4, 22 MUNI bus. Open until 9, Fri–Sat until 10.

Flying Kamikaze's Rock & Roll Sushi. A giant step away from the austerity of most sushi restaurants, Flying Kamikaze's specializes in sake slushes for a well-marinated Marina crowd.... Tel 415/567–4903. 3339 Steiner St. at Lombard St.; 28, 43 MUNI bus. Open until 11, Fri–Sat until midnight.

Fog City Diner. Sleek and warmly lit, this diner across from Levi's Plaza has become one of the emblems of the city. Sit at the plush, posh, polished booths, and order burgers and onion rings or little plates of up-to-the-minute California cuisine.... *Tel 415/982–2000. 1300 Battery St. between Greenwich and Lombard Sts.; 32, 42 MUNI bus. Open until 11, Fri–Sat until midnight.*

Great Eastern. Open late, this noisy, too-brightly-lit Cantonese seafood spot serves up authentic feasts of somewhat scary-looking Chinese cuisine (they'll bring the live, flopping fish right to your table — eek!) as well as more familiar (to Westerners) fare.... *Tel 415/986–2500. 649 Jackson St. between Kearny St. and Grant Ave.; 15, 41 MUNI bus. Open until 1, Fri–Sat until 3.*

Grubstake. After clubbing, sit in an old train car and order great french fries and other diner classics served by outrageously surly waiters. For entertainment, watch the up-past-their-bedtime tourists try to deal with the neighborhood drag queens.... *Tel 415/673–8268. 1525 Pine St. between Polk St. and Van Ness Ave.; 19, 42, 49 MUNI bus. Open until 4. No credit cards.*

Hamburger Mary's. Here's where to chow down on big (beef or tofu) burgers with the club crowd. The Bloody Marys routinely win "Best Of" awards in the free weeklies.... *Tel 415/ 626–5767. 1582 Folsom St. at 12th St.; 12, 42 MUNI bus. Open until midnight, Fri–Sat until 1.*

Hot N' Hunky. Your basic all-American soda-fountain food (burgers, fries, shakes), set in your basic all-American gay neighborhood.... *Tel 415/621–6365. 4039 18th St. at Noe St.; Castro BART/MUNI Metro stop; F streetcar; 24, 33 MUNI bus. Open until midnight, Fri–Sat until 1.*

Icon Byte Bar & Grill. Live worldbeat music, an Internet-wired Apple computer workstation, TV monitors with art-installation, latte-slurping, laptop-tapping cafe society.... Oh yeah, and good low-tech American saloon food—burgers, black bean chili, and salads.... *Tel 415/861–2983. 297 9th St. at Folsom St.; 12, 19, 42 MUNI bus. Open until 10, Fri–Sat until midnight; closed Sun.*

International House of Pancakes. No surprises here: It's exactly like every other IHOP. And some nights, that's a good thing.... *Tel 415/921–4004. 2299 Lombard St.; 28, 43 MUNI bus. Open 24 hours.*

It's Tops Coffee Shop. Since 1947, the best trailer-trash vittles on Market Street after midnight, with homemade pies
and the most generous ice-cream scooper in the city.... *Tel
415/431–6395. 1801 Market St. at Valencia St.; Van Ness
BART/MUNI Metro stop, F streetcar, 37 MUNI bus. Open
Wed–Sat until 3.*

Kan Zaman. Opium-den dining in the Haight: Sit on the floor
under a tent, take a pull of honey-apple tobacco in an enormous hookah, and sip hot spiced wine. Good standard
Middle Eastern fare.... *Tel 415/751–9656. 1793 Haight St.
at Shrader St.; 37, 43, 66 MUNI bus. Open until 11, Fri–Sat
until midnight. No credit cards.*

La Rondalla. With its Christmas lights and mariachi bands, this
is the most festive Mexican eatery in the Mission district....
*Tel 415/647–7474. 901 Valencia St. at 20th St., 26 MUNI
bus. Open until 3:30.*

Lori's Diner. Another faux-fifties diner; Lori's is open round the
clock, and full of revelers after last call. Warning: Lori's is so
brightly lit, you might want to bring shades.... *Tel 415/392–
8646. 336 Mason St. between O'Farrell and Geary Sts.;
Powell BART/MUNI Metro stop; F streetcar; 3, 8 MUNI bus.
Open 24 hours.*

LuLu. A dramatic blue-and-gray grand cafe (soaring skylit ceiling, split-level seating, massive wood-burning oven) with a
memorable Mediterranean menu. For dessert: chocolate
cake, with a lava flow of melted chocolate from its still-
warm center.... *Tel 415/495–5775. 816 Folsom St.
between 4th and 5th Sts.; 12, 27 MUNI bus. Open until
10:45, Fri–Sat until 11:45.*

Max's Opera Cafe. At this glitzy deli near the opera house, one
sandwich is big enough for both of you. Be prepared for
ambush serenades from the singing waitstaff.... *Tel 415/
771–7300. 601 Van Ness Ave. at Golden Gate Ave.; Van
Ness BART/MUNI Metro stop; F streetcar; 42, 47, 49 MUNI
bus. Open Mon until 10, Tue–Thur until midnight, Fri–Sat
until 1, Sun until 11.*

Mel's Drive In. More fun fake-fifties, with coin-op jukes at every
table, hometown-made Bud's ice cream, and the Mel-

burger.... *Tel 415/921–3039. 2165 Lombard St. between Steiner and Fillmore Sts.; 28, 43 MUNI bus. Open Sun–Wed until 2, Thur until 3, Fri–Sat 24 hours. No credit cards.*

Miss Pearl's Jam House. Jam, as in Jamaican: A tropically funky, noisy, spicy, Caribbean/soul kitchen next door to the Phoenix, S.F.'s rock star hotel. Chef Wesley Saunders specializes in what he calls "New-World barbecue".... *Tel 415/775–5267. 601 Eddy St. between Larkin and Polk Sts.; 19, 31 MUNI bus. Open Wed–Thur until 10, Fri–Sat until 11.*

Mitchell's Ice Cream. Family-run ice-cream stand with amazing, exotic flavors.... *Tel 415/648–2300. 688 San Jose Ave. at 29th St., 26 MUNI bus. Open until 11. No credit cards.*

Moose's. Under the sign of an enormous purple-neon Moose is this crowded, noisy, and inconsistent North Beach see-and-be-scene pizza-and-pasta restaurant. The slightly edgy attitude is "we're cool, and you'd better be, too".... *Tel 415/989–7800. 1652 Stockton St. between Union and Filbert Sts.; 15, 39, 41 MUNI bus. Open until 11, Fri–Sat until midnight.*

North Beach Pizza. Arguably the best pizza in the city (but why argue about pizza?), and they deliver 24 hours a day, God bless 'em.... *Tel 415/433–2444. 1499 Grant Ave. at Union St.; 39, 41 MUNI bus. Open until 1, Fri–Sat until 3. Delivery 24 hours.*

Orphan Andy's. This unpretentious, inexpensive Castro all-nighter never closes, and serves up homey diner food at red vinyl booths. Someone will usually talk to you, whether you want them to or not. There's a line after the clubs close.... *Tel 415/864–9795. 3991 17th St. at Market St.; Castro BART/MUNI Metro stop; F streetcar; 24, 37 MUNI bus. Open 24 hours. No credit cards.*

Pasta Pomodoro. Good, fresh pasta in a spiffy, speedy eat-in or take-out atmosphere.... *Tel 415/474–3400, 2027 Chestnut St. at Fillmore St. (in the Marina); 22, 30 MUNI bus. Tel 415/399–0300, 655 Union St. between Columbus Ave. and Powell St. (in North Beach); 15, 39, 41 MUNI bus. Open until 11.*

Pizza Love. The pizza's not great, but hey, it's close to the clubs and it's open late.... *Tel 415/252–5683. 1245 Folsom St.*

between 8th and 9th Sts.; 12, 42 MUNI bus. Open Sun–Wed until midnight, Thur until 2, Fri–Sat until 4.

Polly Ann Ice Cream. The city's strangest but most endearing ice-cream parlor, with a roulette wheel to help you decide among today's unheard-of flavors.... *Tel 415/664–2472. 3142 Noriega St. between 38th and 39th Ave., 71 MUNI bus. Open until 10.*

Postrio. Splurge time: Wolfgang Puck came up from L.A. and created a buzz restaurant with a Californian/Mediterranean menu—and great thin, crisp pizzas, of course.... *Tel 415/ 776–7825. 545 Post St. between Mason and Taylor Sts.; 2, 3, 4, 76 MUNI bus. Reservations necessary, jacket/tie preferred. Open until 10, Thur–Sat until 10:30.*

Rubicon. Yeah, this clubby, industrial (but somehow old-Hollywood-feeling) Cal-Italian restaurant is backed by a troika of movie guys. But Planet Hollywood this ain't, thanks to the real star, chef Traci des Jardins. Sit downstairs, not in the Siberian upper level.... *Tel 415/434–4100. 558 Sacramento St. between Sansome and Montgomery Sts.; Montgomery BART/MUNI Metro stop; F streetcar; 1, 42 MUNI bus. Reservations and jackets required. Open until 10, Fri–Sat until 10:30; closed Sun.*

Slow Club. The fast-track crowd feels most at home in this half-lit, shadowy, post-industrial Mission–Potrero Hill club with excellent, eclectic Californian/Mediterranean eats.... *Tel 415/241–9390. 2501 Mariposa St. at Hampshire St.; 27, 33 MUNI bus. Open until 11:30.*

Sparky's. A pink-neon and black-Formica all-night joint, popular with the after-hours and post-club crowd. The pink light makes everyone look good, even at this hour.... *Tel 415/621–6001. 242 Church St. near Market St.; Church St. BART/MUNI Metro stop, J Church and F streetcars, 22 MUNI bus. Open 24 hours. Delivery until 4am Fri–Sat; until 3am Sun–Thur.*

Stars. Big food, big prices, big time: Celeb chef Jeremiah Towers (whose name is a synonym for California cuisine) has the number-one restaurant in the city, a favorite of the old S.F. society, see-and-be-seen bunch, and the other bunch that likes to watch them.... *Tel 415/861–7827. 150 Redwood St. at Van Ness Ave.; Van Ness BART/MUNI Metro stop; F* streetcar; 5, 42 MUNI bus. Open until 11, Fri–Sat until 11:30. Closed Sun.

Stars Cafe. Stars' quicker, cheaper kid sister lives right around the corner from the opera house and Symphony Hall.... *Tel 415/861–4344. 500 Van Ness Ave. at McAllister St.; Van Ness BART/MUNI Metro stop; F streetcar; 5, 42 MUNI bus. Open until midnight (hours vary with performances).*

The Stinking Rose. "We season our garlic with food" is this touristy-but-good Italian spot's motto and gimmick. The memory of the restaurant will remain with you for days, at least.... *Tel 415/781–ROSE. 325 Columbus Ave. between Broadway and Vallejo St.; 15, 41 MUNI bus. Open until 11, Fri–Sat until midnight.*

Take Orders. "A casual military restaurant" in the Mission, with camouflage decor inside and out. Wear a uniform, receive a free glass of wine with your meal.... *Tel 415/626–5523. 3122 16th St. at Valencia St.; 22, 26 MUNI bus. Open until 3.*

Taqueria Pancho Villa. The line moves fast in this spacious burrito factory, and the assembly line is fun to watch. Try one of the fresh fruit punches.... *Tel 415/864–8840. 3071 16th St. between Mission and Valencia Sts.; 22, 26 MUNI bus. Open until midnight.*

Taqueria Zapata. The burritos are on the bland side, but the people-watching is spicy at this Castro corner cruise spot. Big tables encourage sitting with strangers.... *Tel 415/861–4470. 4150 18th St. at Collingwood St.; Castro BART/MUNI Metro stop; F streetcar; 33, 35 MUNI bus. Open until midnight. No credit cards.*

Ti Couz. Are crêpes the yuppie burrito? Nobody does them better than this charming bit of Brittany in the Mission. Try a glass of draft cider instead of wine.... *Tel 415/252–7373. 3108 16th St. at Valencia St.; 22, 26 MUNI bus. No reservations. Open until 11, Sun until 10.*

Tommy's Joynt. This cafeteria-style hofbrau, a San Francisco fixture, serves buffalo stew, bean-and-bear stew, and sandwiches and beers from all over. But it's a bit like eating at a stadium.... *Tel 415/775–4216. 1101 Geary St. at Van Ness Ave.; 38, 42 MUNI bus. Open until 1:45. No credit cards.*

2223 Market Restaurant. At last, a classy neighborhood restaurant in the Castro.... *Tel 415/431–0692. 2223 Market St.; Church St. BART/MUNI Metro stop, F streetcar, 37 MUNI bus. Reservations recommended. Open until 11, Sun until 10.*

Vicolo. Near the opera house and Symphony Hall, here's where you get your quintessential California pizza on cornmeal pie crust.... *Tel 415/863–2382. 201 Ivy St. between Franklin and Gough Sts.; Van Ness BART/MUNI Metro stop, F streetcar, 21 MUNI bus. Open Sun–Tue until 10, Wed–Thur until 10:30, Fri–Sat until 11:30.*

Vivande. The brick oven, the frescoes, the striped orange-and-ivory lampshades, the ribald murals in the rest rooms.... This Tuscan trattoria is a must-see, and Carlo Middione's Southern Italian cooking is a must-taste.... *Tel 415/673–9245. 670 Golden Gate Ave. between Van Ness Ave. and Franklin St., at Opera Plaza.; Van Ness BART/MUNI Metro stop, F streetcar, 42 MUNI bus. Open until midnight.*

Washington Square Bar & Grill. North Beach central for the older, crabbier San Francisco cigarette-smoking crowd. Fresh fish, classic meat dishes, pasta, and piano jazz.... *Tel 415/982–8123. 1707 Powell St. at Union St.; 15, 39, 41 MUNI bus. Open until 10:30, Fri–Sat until 11:30.*

Zuni Cafe. An archetypal S.F. restaurant, and a temple of Cali cuisine with Italian and Southern French accents. Great oysters and roast chicken, and margaritas at the long copper bar or by the adobe fireplace. Some people hate its "you're lucky that you're here" attitude, though.... *Tel 415/552–2522. 1658 Market St. at Franklin St.; Van Ness BART/MUNI Metro stop, F streetcar, 37 MUNI bus. Open until midnight Tues–Sat, until 11pm Sun. Closed Mon.*

down
and
dirty

All-night pharmacies... For aspirin to head off that hangover, or to fill that prescription you forgot about until after last call, try **Walgreens 24-Hour Prescription Service** (tel 415/861–3136, 498 Castro St.; tel 415/931–6417, 3201 Divisadero St.).

Babysitters... First, ask the concierge if your hotel offers child care service. If not, **American Child Care Service** (tel 415/285–2300) can come to your hotel room, offering excursions to children 12 and older. **Starr Belly Child Care Services** (tel 415/642–1950; pager 415/207–2558) will also come right to your hotel, with 24-hour on-call, CPR-trained providers. Both agencies are licensed, bonded, and insured.

BART... **Bay Area Rapid Transit** is basically a commuter rail system, linking eight stations in San Francisco with the surrounding municipalities. Trains stop running at midnight, so don't plan on cruising in from Oakland at 3am. The price of your trip depends on its length; buy your tickets from the machines at stations. For transit groupies who love to ride the rails but don't have a destination in mind, a $2.60 excursion fare allows you to explore the BART system as far as you care to, in any direction, as long as you exit from the same station at which you entered. For more information, call 415/992–2278.

Buses... Fares for **San Francisco Municipal Railway (MUNI) buses** are $1 for adults, 35¢ for children and seniors. The front of the bus bears its line number and destination. Most service ends at 1am, but about 10 MUNI lines run around the clock. You can buy a route map for $2 at newsstands and other stores. For schedule information, or to find out which line to take to get to a particular destination, call 415/673–MUNI.

Car rental... You can lay out $850 a day and $2 a mile to cruise the town in a Ferrari from Sunbelt Sports Cars, or you can spend about $20 a day for an econobox that comfortably seats a slim family with excellent spatial-relations skills. If you prefer something in between, economy cars run around $30 to $40 per day with unlimited mileage, sportier wheels like a Mazda Miata run closer to $80. Following are some of the many rental companies in San Francisco (most have more than one location): **A-One Rent-A-Car** (tel 415/771–3977, 4343 O'Farrell St.); **Alamo Rent-A-Car** (tel 415/882–9440, 687 Folsom St.); **Avis Rent-A-Car** (tel 800/331–1212, 415/885–5011, 675

Post St.); **Bay Area Rentals, Cars, Trucks and Vans** (tel 415/621–8989, 229 Seventh St.); **Budget Rent-A-Car** (tel 800/527-0700, 415/875–6850, 321 Mason St.); **California Compacts Rent-A-Car** (tel 800/954–7368, 415/871–4421, 245 S. Airport Blvd.); **Dollar Rent-A-Car** (tel 800/800–4000, 415/244–4130, San Francisco International Airport); **Enterprise Rent-A-Car** (tel 800/325–8007, 415/441–3369, 1133 Van Ness Ave.); **Hertz Rent-A-Car** (tel 800/654–3131, 415/771–2200); **Reliable Rent-A-Car** (tel 415/928–4414, 349 Mason St.); **Sunbelt Sports Cars** (tel 415/771–9191, 320 O'Farrell St.); **Thrifty Car Rental** (tel 800/367–2277, 415/788–8111, 520 Mason St.).

Chauffeurs... If taking a taxi seems too plebeian for your night on the town, try **We Drive U, Inc.** (tel 800/773–7483, 415/579–5800), or **Drivers Exclusive** (tel 800/288–6261) for 24-hour service, and you can give your best shot at reenacting a scene from *The Godfather*, or maybe *No Way Out*.

Emergencies... As in most places, **call 911**. Other emergency numbers include: **Ambulance** (tel 415/931–3900); **Poison Control Center** (tel 415/476–6600); **Suicide Prevention** (tel 415/221–1424); and **Traveler's Aid** (tel 415/255–2252).

Events hotline... San Francisco's **Visitor Information Center** runs recorded messages all day and night, listing daily events and activities in English (tel 415/391–2001), French (tel 415/391–2003), Spanish (tel 415/391–2122), Japanese (tel 415/391–2101), and German (tel 415/391–2004).

Festivals and special events...

February: Ring in the Year of the Ox at the **Chinese New Year Celebration** (tel 415/982–3000, parade runs from Market and Second Sts. to Columbus Ave.), the largest festival in a city of festivals.

March: The **San Francisco Asian American International Film Showcase** (tel 415/863–0814, AMC Kabuki 8 Theatre, Fillmore and Post Sts.) features over 100 full-length and short films from around the world. Keep warm at the **Textile Arts Film Festival** (tel 415/750–3627, M. H. de Young Museum, Golden Gate Park, near Tenth Ave. and Fulton St.), which shows a number of Academy Award–winning films pertaining to the use of various textiles. Believe it or not, the revelry of the **St.**

Patrick's Day Parade (tel 415/661–2700, parade runs from the Civic Center to Spear St.) continues well into the night.

April: For a month, beginning in April, **Spike and Mike's Festival of Animation** (tel 415/957–1205, Palace of Fine Arts Theater, Bay and Lyon Sts.) serves up a variety of impressive and disturbing animated works. The **San Francisco Giants' baseball season** swings into action in April at 3Com Park, still known to locals as Candlestick (tel 800/SF-GIANT for tickets). America's oldest film festival, the **San Francisco International Film Festival** (tel 415/929–5000, various locations) screens films and videos from more than 30 countries over several weeks.

May: The **KFOG Sky Concert** (tel 800/733–6318, Justin Herman Plaza) includes a fireworks display. The **Bay to Breakers Weekend** includes not only the eponymous costume footrace on Sunday, but a Friday kickoff party and a Saturday pasta-fest and concert. Mardi Gras madness strikes when **Carnaval** (tel 415/824–8999) hits the Mission district late in the month.

June: The **Union Street Spring Festival of Arts and Crafts** (tel 415/346–9162, Union St.) is a two-day affair featuring food, street performers, a waiter's race, a swing dance contest, and more. San Francisco's oldest street fair, the **North Beach Festival** (tel 415/403–0666, Grant Ave. and Green St.), offers live entertainment, arts and crafts, and other things you might expect from a street fair. More than 350 films and videos from around the world show at the **San Francisco International Lesbian and Gay Film Festival** (tel 415/703–8650, Castro Theatre, 429 Castro St., and other locations) in late June.

July: It's the Big Easy without the overwhelming heat at the **New Orleans by the Bay** festival (tel 415/967–3000, Shoreline Amphitheatre, Mountain View), a celebration of Louisianan culture and heritage, with an emphasis on— what else?—food and music. Watch the skies light up at the *San Francisco Chronicle* **Fourth of July Waterfront Festival** (tel 415/777–8498, Fisherman's Wharf), which complements the de rigueur fireworks display with other entertainment, food, and so forth. Two great tastes go great together at the **Jazz and Wine Festival** (tel 800/733–6318, Embarcadero Center) at the end of the month.

August: The **San Francisco Fair** (tel 415/703–2729, Civic Center) at the end of the month includes music, food, and such native competitions as "Fog Calling" and the "Impossible Parking Space Race." In nearby Sausalito, the **Sausalito Art Festival** (tel 415/332–3555) features thousands of original pieces of fine art.

September: Experimental theater breaks down the fourth wall, and numerous other things it seeks to break down, at theaters throughout downtown San Francisco during the **San Francisco Fringe Festival** (tel 415/931–1094). Multicultural entertainment, including dancing, martial arts, and arts and crafts, highlight the **Chinatown Autumn Moon Festival** (tel 415/982–6306) as the seasons change. At month's end, shuffle down to the **San Francisco Blues Festival** (tel 415/979–5588, Justin Herman Plaza and Fort Mason).

October: The **Castro Street Fair** (tel 415/467–3354, Castro district) fills this predominantly gay neighborhood with live entertainment, food, and a variety of other festivities. The local celluloid scene has its showcase in the annual **Film Arts Festival** (tel 415/552–FILM, Roxie Cinema, 3117 16th St.), which screens low-budget features, documentaries, and experimental shorts by Bay Area filmmakers.

November: The **Dorothy Hamill Ice Skating Center** (tel 800/733–6318, at Embarcadero Center) opens up in November for daily skating. At the end of the month, the **San Francisco Ballet Family Holiday Festival** offers performances of the *Nutcracker* and other family entertainment.

December: Fulfill your New Year's resolution to exercise without interfering with the rest of your revelry at **First Run** (tel 415/668–2243), a midnight two-mile walk and run that begins and ends at Crissy Field.

Gay and lesbian resources... Because of a large and active community, there is no shortage of resources for gays and lesbians in the Bay Area. The **Gay/Lesbian/Bisexual/Transgendered Switchboard** (tel 510/841–6224) operates out of Berkeley. **Dial-A-Dyke** (tel 415/241–1564) is a 24-hour, free bulletin board for lesbians. The **Deaf Gay and Lesbian Center** (tel 415/266–9944 TDD, 800/735–2922 for Cal Relay voice callers) offers news and community-events updates by phone. The **Gay and Lesbian Historical Society** (tel 415/626–0890) collects items of historical signficance; their archives are open on weekends from 2 to 5pm by appointment. The **Names Project** (tel 415/882–5500) administers the AIDS memorial quilt, which now includes more than 26,000 panels. On TV, **Electric City Network** (Fri 10:30pm, cable channel 53) offers gay-oriented programming, and **Lavender Lounge** (Tue 10pm, cable channel 47) is a gay variety show.

Liquor laws... The drinking age, of course, is 21. Packaged alcoholic beverages are sold at liquor and grocery stores, as well as some drugstores, seven days a week. Because California law prohibits the sale of alcohol between 2 and 6am, last call comes at around 1:30, and many night crawlers take the wise precaution of procuring enough beverages for the later hours before Mickey's little hand hits the two.

MUNI Metro streetcars... The streetcars you recognize from decades of Americana operate on five lines, running underground downtown and on the surface elsewhere. Fares are the same as for buses—$1 for adults, 35¢ for children and seniors. Service generally runs until 12:30am; be aware, though, that continual construction has ended service as early as 10pm. Call MUNI information at 415/673–6864 for service information.

Newspapers, fanzines, weeklies... Of the English-language publications in the Bay Area (there are more than 30 foreign-language publications) the main dailies are the *San Francisco Chronicle* and the *Examiner*. These two combine for a single paper on Sundays—look for the "Datebook," a pink insert which serves as a good general guide for tourists, with book reviews and coverage of movies, dance, theater, and museums. A corps of local weeklies, including the *SF Weekly* and *Bay Guardian*, do what weeklies do best—provide better entertainment listings than what you'll find in the dailies. *SF Weekly* has more attitude and a more eccentric, personal approach than the other papers; this is where you'll find listings for performance art, fringe theater, and other only-in-S.F. events. The *Guardian* has more comprehensive listings, but it's more mainstream. Look for pop-culture critic Johnny Huston (who contributed to The Club Scene in this book) in the *Guardian*; also check out Silke Tutor's nightlife column "Nightcrawlers" and Paul Reidinger's pieces on movies and food in *SF Weekly*. The *San Francisco Sentinel* and the *Bay Area Reporter* are both free weeklies, and the best-known gay publications in town; both offer detailed listings of organizations and events.

SAN FRANCISCO ◁ DOWN AND DIRTY

The free weeklies can be found at various bars, bookstores, cafes, and stores around town. To find more from the gay scene, try *Odyssey*, a biweekly zine (in the sense that it comes out every other week) rife with scurrilous Hollywood gossip, as well as contributions from the locally famous drag nuns known as the Sisters of Perpetual Indulgence, who write about anything that crosses their unholy path. *Oblivion*, a monthly gay-oriented magazine, covers clubs (including deejay listings), restaurants, and adult entertainment with a queer slant.

Online info... Even if the best waves are further south, you can trade your surfboard for a motherboard and surf the Net. Here are a few places of interest on San Francisco's leg of the information superhighway. **Snack Cake** is a local webzine which has features, interviews, and columns with a stress on the local and national music scene. The **Haight Ashbury Free Press** features pieces on music and politics, as well as "Groovy Graphics"—just in case you were confused as to where this webzine is based. You can also find news and views from the Haight as well as other San Francisco neighborhoods at the **City Voice** (http://www.blackiris.com/cityvoice/cvhome.html). Football fans have a choice: they can pay homage to the 'Niners at the **Official 49ers Home Page** (http://www.sf49ers.com) or vent their bitterness about the team at the home page of the **49er-Haters Society** (http://www.scruznet.com/~nhs/49hater.html). Hockey fans can visit the home page of the International League's **San Francisco Spiders** (http://www.sfspiders.com/sfspiders). The **Bay Area Art Source** (http://www.foggy.com/indexf.html) offers links to galleries, artists, museums, and other arts venues and events. The **Fine Arts Museums of San Francisco** have a home page at http://www.famsf.org. For **club and live music performance listings**, you can visit http://www.netcom.com/~skipmc/sfclubs.html; for **rave and party information** around San Francisco, try http://207.67.198.21/JMEACHAM. You can dig up more music information at a site kept by **Live 105**, a local alternative music radio station (http://www.live105.com/live105), or at the calendar for the **Plough and Stars**, a traditional Irish music venue (http://www.hooked.net/users/dinosaur/plough.html). Finally, if you want to understand the experience of California citizenship, take a look at the **San Francisco Online Voter**

Guide (http://sf95.election.digital.com), which includes candidates' endorsement lists, ballot statements, campaign finance information, and platform papers, and the text of California's perpetually infamous propositions, with analysis—enough to fatigue even the most civically dedicated citizen.

Parking... First things first: Know how to park on a hill. San Francisco isn't Kansas, and if you don't **curb your wheels**, your car might roll all the way there. Turn your front tires toward the street when your car is pointing uphill, and toward the curb when it's facing downhill. This isn't just good advice; it's the law. When parking on the street, avoid being towed by learning the color-coded curb markings: **red** means no stopping or parking; **yellow** means all commercial vehicles may stop for up to 30 minutes; **yellow-and-black** means only commercial trucks may stop for up to 30 minutes; **blue** means the space is reserved for cars with California disabled placards; **green** means all vehicles may stop for up to 10 minutes; and **white** means that all vehicles can stop for no longer than 5 minutes while the adjacent business remains open. If this seems complicated, quiz yourself. If you slip up, it'll cost you. Minor parking violations run a minimum of $20, plus $100 for towing, plus storage fees. Don't even think of parking in a disabled zone, because your tab will run $250 to $275, not including towing fees. And even if you park illegally for just a few minutes, be warned that the police are vigilant and persistent. Almost 30 percent of all parking tickets issued in the state of California are issued in San Francisco.

If you want to avoid the hassles of street parking, there are plenty of garages in town; prices vary considerably, though. City-run garages tend to be cheaper than privately owned ones, but you should check on availability and rates whenever possible. Overnight parking is available for a mere $3 at the **Sutter-Stockton** (tel 415/982–7275, 444 Stockton St.) and **Ellis-O'Farrell** garages (tel 415/986–4800, 123 O'Farrell St.). Some other garages, listed by neighborhood, include: **Chinatown** (tel 415/956–8106, 433 Kearny St.; tel 415/982–6353, 733 Kearny St.); **Civic Center** (tel 415/863–3187, 355 McAllister St.; tel 415/626–4484, 370 Grove St.); **Downtown** (tel 415/982–8522, 833 Mission St.; tel 415/956–4800, ask for g Mason and Ellis Sts.); **Embarcadero Center** (t

433–4722, 250 Clay St.; tel 415/398–1878, Embarcadero Center Garage); **Fisherman's Wharf** (tel 415/673–5197, 665 Beach St. at Hyde St.); **Japan Center** (tel 415/567–4573, 1660 Geary Blvd.); **Mission District** (tel 415/567–7357, 90 Bartlett St. near 21st St.); **Moscone Center/South of Market** (tel 415/777-2782, 255 3rd St.; tel 415/543–4533, Museum Parc, 3rd and Folsom Sts.); **North Beach** (tel 415/558–9147, 766 Vallejo St.); **Union Street** (tel 415/563–9820, 1910 Laguna St.; tel 415/495–3772, 2055 Lombard St.); **Van Ness** (tel 415/567–9147, 1230 Polk St.).

Radio... Some local stations and their formats: **Live 105**, KITS (105.3 FM), high-profile alternative rock station; **KFOG** (104.5), adult rock; **KALW** (91.7), broadcasts NPR, PRI, CBC, and BBC news, as well as information, public affairs, and music programming; **KKSF** (103.7), a wide variety of jazz; **KMEL** (106), hip-hop, urban pop; **KSAN** (94.9), country; **KDFC** (102.1), classical; **KUSF** (90.3), college station with eclectic music and cultural programming; **KPIX** (95.7) talk radio all day and night, with names like Tom Snyder and Dr. Nancy Snyderman. **Fruit Punch** is a gay radio show that has been on the air since 1973, Wed 7pm, KPFA 94.1 FM and KPFB 89.3 FM; **Hibernia Beach** is a gay talk show, Sun 7am, KITS 105.3 FM.

Taxis... Hailing a taxi on the street is generally fairly easy, particularly in the more touristy areas of town, but if you're operating on a tight schedule, or if you just want to rest your umbrella, you can phone in advance. Just be prepared to wait a good half hour if you call on the busiest of weekend nights. Of the forty-plus taxi companies listed in the Yellow Pages, the most commonly used are **Yellow Cab** (tel 415/626–2345), **City Cab** (tel 415/468–7200), **De Soto** (tel 415/673–1414), **Luxor** (tel 415/282–4141), and **Veteran's** (tel 415/552–1300). Fares are standardized throughout the city: a $1.70 charge rings up when the meter clicks on, and it's 30¢ for every 1/6 mile thereafter.

Time... If the sunrise hasn't come yet to clue you in, you can call 415/767–8900 for the correct time.

Weather... For local area weather any time, call 415/364–7974.